overflowing success

It's Time to Stop Struggling & Enjoy Heaven on Earth...

Where Nothing is Impossible

Todd R. Weaver

Unless otherwise indicated, all Scripture quotations are taken from the HOLY BIBLE, NEW INTERNATIONAL VERSION®. Copyright © 1973, 1978, 1984 Biblica. Used by permission of Zondervan. All rights reserved. Scripture quotations marked "NKJV™" are taken from the New King James Version®. Copyright © 1982 by Thomas Nelson, Inc. Used by permission. All rights reserved.

Overflowing Success: It's Time to Stop Struggling & Enjoy Heaven on Earth...Where Nothing is Impossible

ISBN – 13: 978-1479273591

ISBN – 10: 1479273597

Printed in the United States of America

© 2013 – Todd R. Weaver

All rights reserved. No part of this book may be reproduced or transmitted in any form or by any means, electronic or mechanical, including photocopying, recording, or by an information storage and retrieval system, without permission in writing from the publisher.

Dedication

This book would not exist without my beautiful wife Jodi and our precious son Jacob. This book is dedicated to them. They are truly overflowing success in my life. Jodi is my other half, my partner and my greatest cheerleader. Jacob is the blessed result of our joint prayer. He is the fruit of our love for each other and God's love for us. I love you both very much!

Table of Contents

Introduction vii

Chapter 1   *A Paid-Off Home Mortgage* 1

Chapter 2   *The Blessed Life* 11

Chapter 3   *Success the World's Way* 21

Chapter 4   *There's Just One Problem* 29

Chapter 5   *Our Success Has Already Been Provided* 35

Chapter 6   *Abundance of Love and Grace* 47

Chapter 7   *A Change of Heart* 53

Chapter 8   *Your Vision* 59

Chapter 9   *Preparing for Success* 67

Chapter 10 *Taking Dominion in Your Life* 73

Chapter 11 *Walking Out Success* 83

Chapter 12 *Bring on the Giants* 91

Conclusion 101

About the Author 109

Introduction

Social networking has given us a whole new perspective into people's lives. People freely post whatever pops into their mind. Some can't stop sharing until they have revealed nearly every intimate detail of their lives. If you are active in social media, I am sure that you know what I mean. Don't get me wrong, though. I love staying in touch with people and I do like seeing most of what gets posted. It is fun and it has definitely taken America and the world by storm.

I was surprised, though, by how many negative comments get posted on a daily basis. They seem to far outweigh the positive comments and updates. For example, people seem to anticipate getting extremely sick as soon as they get their first symptom of illness. Sure enough, a few days later you come to find out that they are indeed worse than they were before. Or someone else expects the worst to happen at his or her job. A short time later, it does happen.

Even the casual comments are negative. It seems that people find themselves in a constant state of "going crazy" and being "driven nuts." Not to mention the ever popular "to death" or "dying to" comments…"she was dying to try that!" If people truly think about the words they are using to speak about their lives I would hope that they would decide to change them. Too often we don't value the things we say out loud or type on the computer. Through social media we can watch the results of those words come to pass in their lives. As you have probably noticed, most of what people say ends up happening—both for their good and their not-so-good.

This new media brings into sharper focus the types of negative things people are truly expecting in their lives. Of course they would deny that those things are really what they want. Most of them would say they are just joking. Many times those jokes are used to mask the real pain they are feeling. Keep in mind that this is just what they are willing to share. I don't want to imagine the things they aren't willing to post about their lives. Even if you get the chance to hear someone share more in person or over the phone it can be difficult to hear what is in his or her heart. Sadly, success seems to be a foreign concept in the lives of many. It definitely isn't expected. Survival is the normal way of thinking. When success does occur on occasion, most people think they just got "lucky."

Depression, anger, illness, financial problems—they all bubble up to the surface on our computer screens. Things that used to be hidden are revealed. Obviously we all want to help others. (Perhaps you are one of the people who could use some help.) Many times people will try to post positive responses such as "Keep your chin up!" Others might instead join in with a negative rant of their own. The really sad thing is that it's rare to see an actual solution posted for the problem. Some of the solutions people do offer actually sound worse than the problems themselves. In fact, many people just share that they are dealing with the very same issues.

I see these posts and I know that I have the answer people are looking for. I actually know what they need to succeed. In fact, all of those problems come from just one original problem and so all of those problems have the same one solution. But the answer won't fit in the space you can post a response in. It will take a little more space than that. That's why I wrote this short book. Let me assure you, though, this book has nothing to do with me coming up with the answer on my own. I'm definitely not a self-help guru. Self is what usually gets you into problems, but it isn't what will get you out.

Over the last several years I have received success in just about every area of my life. I am truly blessed. I have titled this book *Overflowing Success* because it gives a great visual for what I mean. It's a flood of goodness coming into your life...success that's too large to contain...success that overflows from your life

Introduction

and into the lives of others. I'm confident that's what this book will do for everyone who reads it. If that sounds good to you, keep reading!

Unlike those negative posts, I actually expect good things to happen to me and my family every day. I also expect that anything that has a slightest look of negativity to it will actually work out for my good. This really has nothing to do with me, with my abilities or with my skills. In fact, my success doesn't even come from me. It is a gift from the Kingdom of God.

Now before some of you stop reading, let me assure you that what I'm talking about here isn't religion. Far from it. In fact, it's completely the opposite of religion. I'm talking about the tangible reality of God in your life today. Of heaven on earth. This isn't the usual "spiritual" answer of not knowing why something negative has happened to you. This also isn't about just surviving "down here" until you go to heaven. I'm taking about a complete change in your current circumstances. I'm talking about real answers and solutions.

My issue was, how do I help those who are struggling? Would they even want to hear the answer? Would they be willing to make the changes necessary to receive success? What if only one person reads this book and finds his or her answer? It will have been well worth it. Maybe you are that person!

This book shows you the way to win in every area of life. We were in fact created to do just that. This is written for anyone out there who is looking to change his or her current situation in life. I assure you that you don't need to remain where you are. God wants His very best for you today. He wants heaven to set up an outpost in your life. Regardless of where you are right now, get ready to rise higher. Get ready to rise far above any challenge you are facing.

Much of what you will read in this book isn't something I came up with. I'm just sharing the changes that have occurred in my life through God's Kingdom. I'm not a pastor and I definitely didn't go to seminary. I have learned much of it by studying some amazing people who have already achieved this success. They have blessed me and now I want to bless you. I know without a shadow of a doubt that this will work for you as it has for me. I also know that once you understand overflowing success you will pass it on to others.

I can also assure you that it is not a coincidence that you are reading this book. I actually heard once that there isn't a Hebrew word for coincidence. It doesn't exist in that language. I believe it. I have seen so many things in my life lately that others would pass off as a coincidence. I know that is not the case. I have seen amazing things happening in the lives of many others too. There are no coincidences. Get ready to start living a coincidence-free life.

CHAPTER 1

A Paid-Off Home Mortgage

My life has radically changed in the past few years. My wife and I became completely debt-free, including our mortgage. We recently had a beautiful, healthy baby boy when we struggled for years to conceive. I haven't been sick in over three years when I used to have illnesses each year. Even our one-year-old baby boy hasn't had a cold. I rarely feel stressed and am truly at peace. Things tend to go my way in all areas. In a nutshell, things are awesome!

Before those amazing changes happened I spent many years feeling stuck. I felt stuck in just about every area of life. That's about the only way I can describe it. I wanted to become unstuck but was unsure where to look for answers. I wanted to live a life that I knew deep inside was available to me.

You probably want a change in your life too, or you might want many changes. Deep inside your spirit you know there is more to be lived in this world and you want to live it. I had that same thought several years ago. My life was good in general. I had a good job and a wonderful wife (she's still wonderful). Many people would have absolutely traded places with me. I just felt something was missing, but I didn't know what it was.

I want to encourage you. What you are looking for is available. In fact, it really is much closer to you right now than you can imagine. This book is written for you. I know it will provide the direction you need. Overflowing success leads to peace, fulfillment, joy, health, financial security and more blessings and miracles than you can count.

Let me say this again. Many of the things I will share with you in this book will be written off as coincidences by the world. Now that you are starting with a coincidence-free mindset, embrace the amazing things that will begin to happen. I have no doubt your life will change in many miraculous ways.

First let me give you a little background on how I first noticed these changes occurring. Several years ago we attended church, but it felt more like an item on the things-to-do list. Don't get me wrong; it was a very good church with some great people in it. But we really felt like we were just going through the motions. Several times we even left the Sunday morning service feeling worse off than before we went in. We weren't expecting much each week and we weren't receiving much.

I remember telling myself one day, "If I really believe what I say I believe, if I really believe in God and that He really sent His Son Jesus to die for me, then there is an answer for me somewhere. If I really had faith, then I shouldn't feel down and I shouldn't feel like I am just going through the motions of life. There should be some real fruit showing up in my life. There should be something to show that I am set apart from the world."

One day I decided that I should be able to find the answer in the Bible. It's God's Word, so the answer I needed had to be in there. I must admit I didn't read the Bible very often. I read the passages mentioned in church and on a rare occasion would read a little on my own. So I picked up my Bible with the intention of figuring out what was missing in my life. It wasn't easy. I read many books each year, but the Bible wasn't an easy read. I was quickly disappointed. The answer didn't just jump off the page at me. I felt let down that there wasn't a flash of revelation at that moment.

However, as I finally really read the Bible, I noticed that it didn't seem to match up with the picture I had in my mind. Jesus kept talking about the Kingdom of God. It seemed to be the focal point of nearly everything He talked about. I had always thought of the Kingdom of God as heaven, a place you go after you die. As I read more, I saw that the Kingdom of God was something that was impacting the earth today. People's lives radically changed when they came in touch with Jesus' Kingdom. All kinds of illness and disease left people. People were returned to their right minds and families had more fish and bread than they could eat. And not only did Jesus transform people's lives, but His followers also transformed people's lives in the same ways. Why wasn't I seeing that today? Why didn't I see change in my own life?

Most of the people in church seemed to have the very same problems as the people outside the church doors. That didn't seem right. Shouldn't they be better off than those struggling on their own? They had God in their life after all. In some ways the people of the church seemed worse off than people of the world. They were sitting back and waiting for God to improve their lives. The people in the world were at least out there trying to improve their lives themselves.

Finding the Answer

Maybe the Kingdom of God was the key? I tried to find any book I could that talked about it. The options were very slim and some of the first books I read weren't all that good. I remember flipping through channels and coming across some pastors on television. Television ministry had always creeped me out as a child. It seemed like a scam and maybe some of the programs were. I hadn't watched anything like that since I was a child. As I watched a few of the pastors, I noticed that some of them were mentioning the Kingdom of God. Maybe I was on the right track, but I didn't expect to learn much from television. Looking back on it, I believe the Holy Spirit was directing me to the answer I was looking for.

Overflowing Success

By just taking that small step of faith and moving forward I started to be led. I would watch some pastors for a short time on television and then move on to another. It seemed like a crash course in God's Kingdom, of learning the basics and then moving on to a new level. I was gaining as much information as I could, as fast as I could.

Eventually I came across a book by a pastor in Singapore named Joseph Prince. The book is called *Destined to Reign*. As I read his book I felt my spirit come alive. The things I read seemed to speak to me as things I had always known, but never actually heard or read before. My eyes were opening to a completely new possibility. Could we really reign in life? Deep down I knew we could. Now this was what I was looking for! I found out that Pastor Prince had a television program on at 5:00 a.m. in America. I began to record his show and watch it almost every day. I was amazed by what I saw. It was as if I was receiving an abundance of God's love and grace every day through this program. It was almost like having my own personal Bible study with Pastor Prince.

I felt years of weight and condemnation washing off me. I actually felt physically lighter. Normal daily life wasn't getting me down like it used to. I slowly began to walk in freedom. Things really started to change for me. My attitude was much better and my relationship with my wife went from very good to very great. Things just seemed to click more on a daily basis. Life was more enjoyable and became more successful. I was actually exerting less effort but seeing greater results. It was just as Joseph Prince describes on his television show: right believing was leading to right living.

I did discover that it couldn't just be a one-time thing. I couldn't watch the show and then take time off. I had to constantly hear the teaching and constantly hear about God's love for me. If I were to take a few days off and not listen to his teaching and not listen to God's Word I would slip back into the old "stuck" feeling. Even to this day I have to feed on the Bread of Life as often as I can. I have to feed on Jesus. It's a daily feeding. The children of Israel fed on the manna in the wilderness. The manna

A Paid-Off Home Mortgage

did not keep for the next day. We too must feed on the Bread of Life daily.

We must feed on the Bread of Life daily.

Questions I had always had about God were being answered. Questions I had about the Bible were being answered. My spiritual life began to come together for the first time. My confidence grew in this Kingdom and how it could impact my life today.

One of the passions my wife and I had was to be completely out of debt. We focused a lot of our time on it. We were able to pay off the credit card debt early in our marriage and had paid off pretty much everything else, including our student loans, before we married. We had moved on to paying off our home mortgage. We did a pretty good job of not overspending, and we cut back where we could. We watched *The Dave Ramsey Show* each week and hoped to call in one day and scream that we were "debt free"! We made a really nice dent in our mortgage, paying off around half of the mortgage amount in our first four years of marriage.

Right around the same time I was changing personally through the information I was receiving about God's Kingdom, I just happened to be looking at the cable television guide and saw a show called *Faith Life Now*. I felt a strong prompting to check it out. I turned the channel and found a couple talking about both being debt-free and the Kingdom of God. Needless to say it was not a coincidence. It was a perfect fit for us. It was as if God designed a television program just for us. It was on at a time of day we aren't normally home and wouldn't normally be watching television. It just so happened that we were both home that day. I told my wife that she had to see this show. It featured a couple named Gary and Drenda Keesee. At the end of the show I said, "Wouldn't it be great if we had a church like that around here?" Just then the credits said that their church was located in Ohio. It was about a forty minute drive from our house. We both looked at each other and said, "I guess we're supposed to check this place out."

I drove by one day looking for the church. I wanted to pick up some of the CDs they mentioned in their broadcast. I saw a beautiful church and pulled up. It was the only church I could find in the area I knew they were located in. But it wasn't their church. I didn't see anything else but an old warehouse. The sign in front of that warehouse said Faith Life Church. Concerned that this might be a scam, I drove away discouraged.

We couldn't stop watching their television show though and continued to love what we were hearing. People's lives were being transformed by the Kingdom of God. We decided to give the old warehouse church a chance. We went one weekend, parked and went in. The sanctuary was dark and small. The people all seemed extremely friendly and unaware that they were in a dark warehouse. The music there was contemporary; we were used to more traditional hymns. The first thirty minutes or more was nothing but praise music. This was something completely new to us. We were both used to a more traditional service. I thought, at first, that maybe someone didn't show up to do the other portions of the service and they were just covering for them with more music. When the message at that service came, it really hit home with us. Our lives can change through the Kingdom of God. And there should be evidence of God in our lives. People should see our success that comes through Him. It should even overflow our lives. My wife and I became excited about the possibilities.

The Kingdom of God Worked!

We kept going to our local church, but we would go to that little warehouse church every now and then. During that time I had hit a rough patch at my job. I was likely to lose my job and if I didn't lose it I was going to have to pick up the extra work of a number of other people who would be let go. I was sure to remain at my current salary even if my workload tripled. Either way it wasn't going to be good. I was extremely stressed. I had been hearing about planting seeds in God's Kingdom at the warehouse church, so I decided that I was desperate enough to try it. I wrote out a check, which was my biggest church donation ever. I'm ashamed to admit it, but I didn't tell my wife that I was doing it until after

A Paid-Off Home Mortgage

the service was over and the check was long gone. It seemed crazy. Why would I write this church in a warehouse (not even my home church) the largest check I had ever given? Why would I do it with the chance I could lose my job and need that money?

I continued to feel stuck at work. Sometimes I thought about the money I had given away. What had I done? One day shortly after that I got my answer. I was told that I was going to lose my job, but I would receive a generous severance package and some additional compensation that is unheard of in my industry. The amount I received was almost fifty times the amount I had given to the church that day. On top of that I received an offer to go to work for a great company right away. So what had been an extremely stressful time turned into an extremely joyous time. I had a wonderful new job and a great payout from my old job. For the first time I saw something tangible result from my faith. It was amazing!

At that same time, my car had over 200,000 miles on it. I was able to buy a very nice used car for cash from a portion of that check. I found one that was only two years old and half the price of a brand-new one. This car had only 24,000 miles on it and was still under warranty, including things like oil changes. I also received an extremely high trade-in value for my old car. People started to call us lucky, but we knew that wasn't the case. We were blessed.

I remember my wife and I looked at each other one day and both said at the same time: "I think we should start going to Faith Life Church full-time." The church had just moved out of the warehouse and into a new state-of-the-art building. It was beautiful and a world away from the building where we first attended the church. We continue to be blessed at this church to this very day.

During this time I began to pick up many of the teachings about God's Kingdom on CD from Gary Keesee, Joseph Prince and others. I listened to them all the time in the car. Between church, the television shows and the CDs I was getting quite an education regarding God's Kingdom. Again, the key was to listen over and over to the teaching to let it really sink in. I needed to let it sink in to both my head and my heart.

Overflowing Success

I believe it was during the first week we started attending the new church full-time that they had a sermon called "The Difference a Year Can Make." It was January and the start of a new year. They challenged us to believe God for something big that year. We both agreed that paying off the remainder of our house in one year was something too big for us to do on our own. We had done a very good job over the previous four years, but we knew there was no way we could pay off the remaining fifty percent in twelve months. We figured we could keep on our current path and pay it off in another four years or so. That would be great, but to pay it off in only twelve more months would be amazing.

We were willing to see what would happen and wrote down that we were "believing God for a paid-off home mortgage in twelve months." We didn't know how it would happen, but as we learned with my job change previously—God was able to do exceedingly more than we could ask or think. So we planted a new seed. This time we asked God to reveal to us what size seed to sow. My wife and I came into agreement with each other about what we were believing God for. We were partners this time.

Over that year we continued to add to the extra amount we were paying on our mortgage each month. We kept stretching and kept increasing the extra amount. My wife's commissions at work also rose significantly. We were also giving more to the church than we had in the past. We kept living roughly the same lifestyle. We didn't really feel like we were lacking. Even though we kept paying more and more on the mortgage, the size of our savings account also kept increasing. The mortgage was shrinking at an amazing rate.

What had changed for us was that we were receiving God's love and believed that He wanted us to pay off our mortgage before the end of the year. We believed it was possible and we acted on that belief.

Needless to say in December of that same year we walked into our mortgage company's office and paid off the remainder of our mortgage. We were so excited! We asked them to take a picture of us. We got a sense that day of how rare paying off a mortgage is,

A Paid-Off Home Mortgage

especially for people in our age group. We are completely debt-free today and can't explain how good it feels.

We give God all the glory for paying off our mortgage that year! He took an impossibility and made it a reality. We had our first major taste of God's Kingdom together as a couple and it has changed our lives. From that point forward we started looking at every situation in our lives from the starting point of God's love for us. Once we knew we were established in His love for us through Christ, we were able to receive His blessings in our lives. We were resting in Him and the blessings He has already provided. We weren't sitting back just hoping God would bless us one day.

> We started looking at every situation in our lives from the starting point of God's love for us.

We love being debt-free and we hope all of you also become completely debt-free. You will discover, like we did, that your finances are a key component to your life. It is the number one thing couples fight over. When you get your finances under control you have a real sense of peace in your household. It's hard to have a household of love when you are constantly in a state of fear about making payments. When you become debt-free—including your mortgage—all sorts of possibilities open up to you and your family. It provides a key component to an amazing life together.

We love living in God's Kingdom and you will too. We took what we learned leading up to our mortgage payoff and use it in all areas of our life now. Finances were just a starting point, but money is the area that seems to have most people trapped. When you are trapped in the world's system you can't get yourself free. The good news is that Jesus has set us free from that system. Most people just aren't enjoying it. When you choose to live from God's system instead, your whole universe changes.

I know what you are thinking. You're glad it worked for us, but it sounds impossible for you. Let me assure you that all things are possible with God. Remove impossibility from your vocabulary. You might not pray today and find your life changed tomorrow.

Many times it is a process. Things are going to need to change in your life to make your dreams a reality. In essence we needed to become the type of people who pay off our mortgage before we ever paid it off. You will need to change who you are. Once you change who you are, it is much easier to walk out those steps to success.

You already know how to succeed. Let's stick with the example of money. You already know how to become debt-free. It is simple. Spend less than you earn, boost your income and use all that money to pay down your debt. If that were easy everyone would be debt-free. So what is it? It is an inward change in your being that moves you along to being debt-free. Along with that inward change you can receive supernatural help from God to get you there.

The Kingdom of God covers everything in your life, not just your finances. It changes your attitude, your health, your relationships—absolutely everything. It changes all of these areas for the better. It brings life to every situation. I don't know what you need in your life right now, but I can assure you that if you need it, it is available in the Kingdom.

CHAPTER 2

The Blessed Life

In the first chapter you got to peek into our lives in recent years. It has been an amazing transformation. As amazing as those things were, they are just highlights of a life that is now full of blessings and miracles. Most of the world is hoping for a miracle to happen just once in their lives. We now expect to receive supernatural success and abundance on a daily basis. I know that can sound arrogant, but it's not meant to be. We are just one hundred percent confident in our heavenly Father and His will for good in our lives. Faith means you expect that good things will constantly flow from our loving Father.

Our loving heavenly Father provides many good things for all of us. It is just a matter of receiving them. He provides favor for us in a variety of situations. He provides direction. He provides answers. He gives us ideas that we need to follow through on. He also hides things from us for us to search them out. By this I mean God has placed things in the earth for us. They are hidden from us and from men. They are hidden from the enemy too. Once we search for them we will find them at just the right time.

Overflowing Success

We expect to receive supernatural success and abundance on a daily basis.

In this chapter I want to share some of the amazing supernatural things God has done recently in our lives. Always keep in mind that God is no respecter of persons—meaning that what He has done for me and my wife He will do for you. And anything He is doing for someone else He will do for all of us.

Money and Weather

When I stepped into the teaching about His Kingdom the doors of blessing opened wide. As I am writing this book the stock market has been in turmoil. The market has been seeing huge swings up and down. When the market had recovered several months back we felt the prompting of the Holy Spirit to get our money out of the market. We ended up pulling it all out within a month of the high of the market. We still have the money from all of those investments even though the market is down sharply from that point.

Miracles can even involve the weather. We live in Ohio and one day we found ourselves in a blizzard. Our neighborhood is huge and we have a large number of people who stop by trying to sell things or trying to get you to sign their petition. So I typically ignore the doorbell when it rings. I know it sounds bad, but you do need to take dominion over your time. Well, something rose up inside of me to say out loud to my wife, "If anyone comes to the door today, in this weather, I'm buying it." Sure enough, within a half hour the doorbell rang and my wife and I just stared at each other. There were several feet of snow drifted up the door. She answered the door and it was someone offering to shovel our driveway for us at a great price. Thank You, Jesus! I had just strained my back recently lifting furniture. We gladly accepted the offer and I sat upstairs watching this "angel" clear our driveway from the comfort of my chair.

We saw that the words we spoke had impact during the blizzard, so we decided to try it again during the worst windstorm we had ever seen in Ohio. My wife and I came into agreement that the wind would not harm our home and we would not lose our electricity (something that was predicted for this storm). The storm hit and our house was fine. Many of the houses in our neighborhood required new roofs. We didn't lose a shingle. After the storm I noticed that the street right behind us was without power and ended up being without it for several days. Our electricity remained on the entire time. Thank You, Jesus!

I also tried this recently with a relative. I had stopped by for a visit and he was concerned about a strong storm that was coming toward his house. We came into agreement that the storm would not harm their house and they would not lose their electricity. I drove home from their house through that same storm and it was bad. (I should have prayed to avoid it myself!) It hit me shortly after I left their house. I could barely see through the rain and I heard tornado sirens going off as I drove. When I got home and called to check in, he said they had blue sky the whole time. Amazing! Our God is so good!

We had family over during another storm recently. The tornado sirens were going off in our neighborhood. I prayed that the storm would not affect our home. As we watched the storm on the radar we could see it break in two sections and actually go around the area where our home is located. Awesome!

On the way to North Carolina for vacation recently there was a remnant of a tropical storm that was heading through the area we were going to. We prayed that rain would not interrupt our vacation. On the way down we drove through a ton of rain; it was not a pleasant drive. We had our raincoats in the car, but we never needed them the whole trip. When we would get out of the car to get gas, etc., the rain would just stop. When we got to our destination we didn't need the coats either. While checking the weather we saw that many of the towns around us got hit with more than ten inches of rain. Where we were staying got just over an inch of rain and none while we were there. My wife overheard someone at the coffee shop say how remarkable it was that this area received so little rain while everyone nearby got drenched.

The Best Parking Spots

We get blessed quite a bit with our cars and parking too. During the past year we were heading to a local festival and knew it would be crowded. Before we left I said, "Thank You, Dad, that we find an amazing parking place at the festival." I was led to take a back way to the festival we normally wouldn't take. As we got close, I thought I had an idea as to where we might get a good spot. We both saw an entrance to a parking lot and thought it was our best option. We pulled in. All of the spots were full, but they directed us to the front of the lot, nearest the entrance to the festival. They actually added a few "extra" non-marked spots and we parked. We ended up with a better parking spot than ninety-five percent of the people who got there well before us. As we walked out of the lot, they closed off the entrance and marked it as full. Perfect timing. The lot we were in was completely different than the one I thought I was going to. When I saw the lot I thought I was in, I saw that it was completely full already. Had I tried to go for that lot, I would have ended up very far from the entrance. I really don't know how we got to the parking spot we did, but I thank God for it. Many times when God blesses you, you won't know how you got there.

My wife is great at getting amazing parking spots. She just thanks Jesus for an amazing parking spot before she gets there and she gets it more often than not. I mean literally the closest spot to the door, in a crowded parking lot, on a consistent basis. I have been doing it lately too and it's amazing. Does God care where you park? Yes, He cares about every hair on your head and every aspect of your life.

Just this week as I was writing this book, my wife's "check engine" light came on in her car for the first time ever. She's up to 75,000 miles on her car and the car is over five years old. She took it into the shop and they gave her a rental car. We came into agreement and prayed that there would be no charge for any repairs that would be needed. The shop called back and said the repairs would be $1,500. Not good, especially right before Christmas. I must admit, I figured we would just pay the $1,500 and move on. My wife held on to her faith and prayer and when the part came in she asked if there was anything they could do. They called her back and said there would be no charge for the repair or the rental car. They were covered by a warranty we knew nothing about. Praise God!

I have seen this type of thing over and over in our lives and heard stories from many others. Sometimes the situation looks dim. Hold on to your faith. Don't waver and push on through. Don't accept the circumstances the world throws at you. There is nothing too hard for your Dad to overcome...He just wants you to believe it.

> There is nothing too hard for your Dad to overcome... He just wants you to believe it.

Finding Lost Items

We also pray for "smaller" things too. I lost my glasses and couldn't find them for days. I only wear them before bed and really didn't want to spend money on a new pair. My wife suggested we come into agreement that we would find my glasses. She suggested that we agree to find the glasses within the next ten minutes (she almost always outdoes me with her faith). Keep in mind I had looked everywhere for days in my own strength already. After we prayed I had a thought pop into my head. I would describe it more as a leading. I walked right upstairs, pulled the bedspread back and found my glasses toward the bottom of the bed between the sheet and the bedspread. I would never have thought to look there on my own.

I'm sure we can agree nothing is too small to bring to God. I came to find out that what happened to me was called a word of knowledge. It's also called revelation knowledge. It's something unknown that is revealed to us by God. We have the mind of Christ and have the ability to receive downloads from heaven with information we could not know in the natural. Sadly we often don't draw on this amazing knowledge, even though it is available.

I had a similar experience with a pair of lost gloves my wife couldn't find. I asked God where they were. The location just sort of popped in my head and I was led to the laundry basket above the dryer. They were located beneath a pile of stuff in that basket. How much time and energy do we waste in this world with mundane tasks such as looking for lost items. God knows where the lost items are. Just ask Him to show you.

Favor for Travel

We love to travel. During one flight I overheard the person at the check-in desk say the airline had no pilots available for our flight and it would likely be canceled. This was not good, since we were only halfway to our destination. I knew by then that I no longer needed to accept what the world threw my way. I praised God under my breath that we would have pilots shortly and our flight would take off soon. The old me would have been thrown into a panic. The new me knows that there is no reason to panic. I just remain at rest. Not long after that the pilots showed up and we were on our way.

In this world your stress level can only be reduced by answers. God has all the answers. When you have God in your life, your stress fades away. Many times we feel these situations are not important enough to get God involved in them. You have not because you ask not. Just ask.

> In this world your stress level can only be reduced by answers. God has all the answers.

A similar thing happened as we were returning on a flight. The jet bridge wouldn't connect with the plane. The announcement indicated that it might be quite a while before it got fixed. It had been a long trip and everyone wanted off that plane. While the other passengers began grumbling, I began praising God and thanking Him that the bridge would connect shortly. It was fixed in just a few short minutes. With God there are no problems.

Faith means praising God before you see the problem corrected. Everyone can praise God after the problem is over, but those of faith need to do it beforehand. See the problem as already resolved in your spirit. As you already know, when the world finds itself in distress it has nowhere to turn. They are helpless. Many also try to pray from a position of fear. That's the opposite of faith. Pray instead from a position of power—His power. We, as the children of God, only need to thank our heavenly Dad. Does He want you to take off on time or to get you off your plane quickly after a long flight? Of course He does. We, as His children, just need to thank Him ahead of time. It's already taken care of.

We had another flight to Florida. I had booked a flight with a connection through Washington, DC for a cruise we were taking. I noticed that another airline was now offering a direct flight. It wasn't available when I first booked our flight. I felt something in my spirit say to buy the direct flight for the return leg. I thought, This is crazy. Why would I buy an extra flight just for the convenience of flying direct on the way home? I had peace to buy the extra flight, so I did. We took the connecting flight down, but we had two flights on the way back. I felt in my spirit that I should get ready to trade in that connecting flight ticket for a free round trip ticket because that plane would be overbooked. Our direct flight was located right across from my other connecting flight's check-in counter. As I saw them reach for the microphone I jumped out of my chair and went straight up to the counter right as they were offering a free round trip ticket for anyone willing to give up his or her seat. I was first in line. I gladly gave up the seats we weren't going to use and finished up the paperwork just in time to catch our direct flight home. We really enjoyed using our free round trip flights!

When the Holy Spirit speaks to you, move. Try to keep yourself in a state of readiness. Not a state of stress, but one of expectation. Be resting, but ready to move at His prompting. He'll let you know when to go, but if you hesitate you might miss the divine appointment.

One of my favorite testimonies of all is during the year we were paying off the last half of our mortgage. It was "The "Difference a Year Can Make" year. I had found a great price on a cruise in Europe. It was only $399 per person for an inside cabin of a weeklong Mediterranean cruise. An amazing price! We wanted to go for our five-year anniversary, but we knew we needed to keep focused on paying off our home. Besides, flights were over $800 a person and I had seen them as high as $1,200 a person. This was more than we could afford. I said out loud, "Dad, if You want us to take this anniversary trip, make it so apparent that we know it is You." The very next day that flight to Barcelona dropped to $260 plus tax round trip. I probably couldn't fly to Florida for that. Sadly I didn't book it right away. I don't know what I was thinking. I couldn't sleep that night. So first thing the next morning I booked the flight. Right after I booked it, the flight cost went right back to up $800. What the world thinks of as a coincidence, we know is a blessing. We had an amazing anniversary trip, thanks to our Dad! How many people get round trip flights from Ohio to Europe for $260? I printed out the page from the website we booked it on and keep a copy of that booked flight in my journal. I'm looking at it right now.

These things have nothing to do with our performance. We didn't behave right to earn these blessings. We didn't earn them at all. They are a gift of right believing. It is resting in the finished work of Christ and knowing He has restored us as sons. We have the entire estate. We are blessed to be a blessing to others. The more that reality flows into your life, the more it flows out of your life and into the lives of others. God wants to use your life as His access point to bless others. To do that we must first be blessed. We are meant to be a river not a lake. You become stagnant if everything that flows into your life just sits there. Let it flow out.

> We are meant to be a river not a lake.

Don't Worry about Missing it

Shortly after my wife had become pregnant she went in for a massage. We were keeping things quiet since it was so early in the pregnancy, so nobody knew yet. There are some massage techniques that aren't safe to do to pregnant women. My wife didn't know that. God was looking out for us as usual. My wife's massage therapist told her that she had a dream that my wife was pregnant the night before her appointment. She explained why it was important that she know if she was pregnant before she started. God is so good!

Sometimes you can miss it, though. This is a great example. When we were paying off the final year of our mortgage during "The Difference a Year Can Make" year, we planted a large financial seed in the church. In fact, it was our largest seed to that point. We were believing God for supernatural assistance in paying off the last half of our mortgage in one year. I went to bed one night and asked God for a sign or direction on what to do. Asking God for an answer right before sleeping has led to a number of great revelations and breakthroughs for us! In the morning my wife said she had a strange dream (she didn't know that I had prayed). She dreamed that she had a certain kind of credit card (that we didn't have). She went to buy something with this credit card and they gave her a large sum of cash along with her purchase. What struck me strange is that this was the middle of the banking crisis. I had read an article recently about that particular credit card company and how it might be a good investment during the downturn. The strange thing was that the current price of that stock was right around the price of the item my wife was buying in her dream. Along with that, the amount of cash they gave back to her in the dream was around the fifty-two week high for the stock.

We discussed buying some of the stock and the amount we thought we might invest. During this time I was listening to a CD and the pastor on it used the slogan for this credit card company in the sermon (although it wasn't intended that way). It just seemed to resonate with my spirit that we should move forward. As a rule we avoid investing in single stocks—did I mention I used to work for Enron? We talked about it, but we never came into agreement as a couple, so we passed on the opportunity.

Overflowing Success

After several months no other major breakthroughs came to us and we were getting close to the end of the year. It is about a week or two before we would be paying off our mortgage and I remember catching a quick look on the TV at that stock we had talked about buying. I felt the Holy Spirit say, "This is the day I would have had you sell that stock." It was back to almost exactly the fifty-two week high again, like in the dream. I ran the math and we would have gained a very nice five-figure sum of money that would have almost exactly paid off the remainder of our mortgage on its own. God made it really easy for us. In fact, we would have ended up with a paid-off home mortgage and a bigger savings account than we started with. We didn't step out in faith on that opportunity. That's okay. We are all learning. We will be better prepared next time.

As I mentioned before there is no word for "coincidence" in the Hebrew language. There are things in motion behind the seen world. God can put you in the right place at the right time to avoid an accident or to get an amazing job offer. One key is to write down all these things that begin happening to you in your journal or in a special notebook. It's too easy to forget them, regardless of how amazing they are. Write down the things you are asking God for and also remember to write down when they arrive. Review the miraculous things God does in your life as a family! You will truly see the mathematical impossibility of all these things randomly happening to you and others.

I had actually been talking about writing this book for a while and felt that the Holy Spirit was prompting me to get started. I said another silent prayer in bed after my wife was asleep, asking if I should write this book. We woke up in the morning and the first thing my wife said was, "What happened with that book you were going to write?" Needless to say I got started on it right away.

CHAPTER 3

Success the World's Way

Now that you have a taste of the Kingdom of God's ways of success, let's take a step back and look at the world's way of doing things. It should be a good starting point to see how you can overcome that system and succeed in every area of life.

We all grew up in the world's system. This was the only option we thought we had. Up until now it has been the only system any of us have ever known. It's normal. For example, if you are short on money, you use a credit card. If you have a problem, you seek an expert from the world to solve it for you. Things tend to be a struggle. It's a continuous cycle. Problems come up. You struggle to find a solution. You get back on your feet and another problem comes along. There is no winning in that system.

Let's be honest, though. We have all tried to get ahead the world's way. We have all tried to beat that system. For example, we are told to study hard in school, get good grades and get a good job. I did that in college. I studied, worked pretty hard and left college with a 3.93 GPA. I also graduated with the Outstanding Senior and Outstanding Marketing Student awards. I sat back and waited for the job offers to roll in. Talk about self-righteousness.

The bad news was that I graduated during a recession. No amazing offers came in and I ended up having to move home with my parents. I felt defeated. I felt I did what I was supposed to do according to the world's way of doing things, yet I was no better off than those who didn't push themselves. Obviously I'm not saying not to work hard or get good grades. I'm just saying that isn't the true answer.

Trying the World's System

So I decided to do more of what the world said to do. I turned it up a notch, as they say. I read hundreds of wealth books. I realized that nobody was going to hand me success just because I had a strong GPA. I was going to have to go out there and take it myself. There are people who had already succeeded and I could gain their entire lifetime of knowledge in one small book. As a Christian, though, I always thought God would just bless me because, once I succeeded, I would give more than someone else would. Needless to say that never happened. I recently gave away many of those books. Please don't get me wrong—many of those books contained some good information, and I did keep some. The basic premise in most of them was to find a good idea and sacrifice everything to make it become reality. That's the way many "self-made" people do it. I just kept thinking that there had to be a better way.

I learned that there is wisdom in the world. It's better than operating without any wisdom at all. In the end, though, it always leads to less than the best that God wants for you. Even if some successful person seems to have a great life on the surface, many times something less than desirable is going on behind the scenes.

You always lose something in the world's system in order to gain something. You might sacrifice meeting your husband or wife in order to "get to the top." Or you might sacrifice having children in order "to get to the top." Or if you do have a spouse and children, you might sacrifice any meaningful time with them in order to "get to the top." Then when you think you "got to the top," you end up losing it all anyway. The world's system is a lot like gambling. If you play long enough you will eventually lose it all.

You always lose something in the world's system in order to gain something.

I did get a few peeks at the top for myself, though. Throughout my career I had the opportunity to work with some of the world's wealthiest and most successful people. I discovered what we already know deep down inside: the people at the top are just like everyone else; they just have more money. I've heard it said that money simply makes you more of what you already are. That's probably true. Deep down I knew that clawing my way to the top wasn't for me. If I followed the world's system, "won" the game and made it to the top—what then? The people at the top have the same problems as the rest of us, but they do have one advantage. They have more money to try to solve their problems the world's way. So while life is easier at the top, it isn't necessarily better.

Being poor is definitely a disadvantage to being rich when you are in the world's system. When you are poor you have no wealth to trust in, and the only thing the world's system has to trust in is its wealth. Just because someone doesn't have money doesn't mean money doesn't have his or her heart. They are probably thinking about money just as much as or more than a wealthy person does.

You will also meet or hear about people who choose to live a life of poverty. They choose to live a meager existence. It may sound nice on the surface but it isn't truly living. Whenever you choose to live below your full potential you are cutting off others from being blessed. As weird as it sounds, you are being selfish. When you limit yourself to receiving handouts from others, you make yourself one less person who can impact the world for good. You are created to be so much more than that!

But this is the world that we live in. It's a world filled with self-effort, a world filled with self-righteousness. All that stress! This world is also full of depression. It is full of ups and downs. It is about striving to get to a fictional level of success where everyone is happy and all of your problems go away.

Think about the popular television shows we watch. Most of them are about the drama in, and collapse of, other people's lives. From "reality" shows to talk shows, they are almost all the same. I guess watching them just makes us feel better about our own lives.

The World's Keys to Success

As I said before, most people think that working hard is the key to success. I know a lot of people who work hard and barely get by. You probably do too, You might even be one of them! In fact, most of you have probably noticed that the people who do most of the work are stuck while others are promoted above them. Why would anyone want to promote the people who are getting the work done? Then nothing would ever get done.

People eventually learn that hard work is not the key to success. Then they move up to another level, which is "playing the game." This is the "who you know" or "who you can get to know" level. What party do you need to get an invite to? Maybe someone you know can put in a good word to get your child into the right school. Playing the right game gets you in position to "win" better than hard work ever does, right?

Some even take it a step further and choose to do whatever it takes to "win." They might lie; they might use people; they might cheat. If you are relying on your self-effort alone, you will look for any advantage you can find. Survival of the fittest turns into a game of "anything goes" very quickly.

Of course, almost everyone has seen the infamous "corporate ladder" and tried to climb it. Sure, there are examples of where doing your best can get you up a rung or two, but eventually you run out of steam. You probably figure things will be great if you can just get that new job. All your problems will magically go away if you just get that next promotion. Success is always just beyond the horizon and you never actually enjoy the place you are in right now.

Let's say you do finally get that promotion. You finally make it up a few rungs. Sure, you could finally pay off that four-year-old car or pay an additional amount each month on the mortgage of the house you currently own, but what fun is that? Now you can afford payments on a bigger house and a newer car. You worked too hard to continue to drive that junker and live in your current house. You deserve more. You worked too hard to get there. It's the price of success, right? Otherwise what's the point in succeeding?

You'll quickly find that there is no peace when you achieve things through your own self-effort. You will always be looking over your shoulder at the next person willing to do whatever it takes to knock you off your perch. You never really enjoy the position you have reached. If you achieve it on your own, you need to maintain it on your own. You have to defend it on your own. You never truly rest.

> There is no peace when you achieve things through your own self-effort.

In the end, most people work their whole lives to finally reach retirement. This is the magical land of rest for most of the world. What often happens? Many times people die shortly after they reach retirement because they have finally reached their goal. Or they might deteriorate more slowly over time watching golf on TV. That's no way to live. God wants you to experience your best life each and every day right now! In fact, I'm told there is no word for "retirement" in the Hebrew language also, just like there is no word for "coincidence." Are you starting to see a pattern forming? If there is no word for it, it probably doesn't truly exist. It's a mirage that draws people across the desert only to disappear in front of them.

What Does Worldly Success Look Like?

Let's take a quick look around the neighborhood. Have you seen the "keeping up with the Jones'" lifestyle? Everyone needs a new car, even if it leased—even if one has continued to roll negative equity from the previous car into the next one and the next one. Everyone wants the latest and the greatest. Debt is just the assumed lifestyle. We have all been there.

What about health? Many are in a constant state of stress, never able to rest. Their nerves might be shot. They might even sacrifice their health with workaholism in the hopes that they might one day make some real money. As many have pointed out, they end up spending all that money to regain the health they once had.

What about relationships? Their spouse knows they work late so they can get the things they both want, right? How else are they going to pay for that house? Even though they don't have much time to talk, the wife knows the husband is doing it for her and the kids, right? And of course they want a better life for their children than the life they had. They enroll their children in every class available, hoping to make them more rounded. Their children dance, play every sport under the sun, sing, cheer and go to every summer camp there is. These families spend their weekends stressed out and driving from tournament to tournament. Then they barely get any sleep and start the work week exhausted again on Monday.

So then what happens? They tell their kids the same thing you were told: work hard, get good grades and get a good job. The cycle starts all over for them too. We need to break that cycle. We need to know that there is more to life than the rat race. Generation after generation of us have been living under this curse.

Inside the walls of many churches it isn't much better. People are exhausted from their work week and spend most of their evenings and weekends running around from church activity to church meeting to church social. They have simply transferred their "work hard to succeed" attitude from the world to the church. This time the CEO is God and they feel they must move up the corporate church ladder to feel "successful" in their spiritual life. This is a counterfeit to the real life God wants for His people. We are transferring the broken system of the world into our church life.

Success the World's Way

As a Christian I thought that I could pray and bam! I would receive the miracle I was looking for. I would receive the success I was striving for. My pastor calls it "mailbox mentality." You hope one day, out of the blue, God will have a check show up in your mailbox and all of your problems will disappear. After all, you are a good person. You don't step on or use other people. You will actually help others when you hit it big. I waited for that to happen for decades.

Ah, but what if you could just win the lottery? That would take care of all your problems, right? All your bills would be paid. You wouldn't owe anyone anything. You could finally rest once and for all.

Sadly, it seems like most of the lottery winners end up worse off than they were before. Many of them are broke. Many of their families can't stand to be around them. Many of their marriages are over. I thought money was supposed to solve those problems. If more money alone were the solution, shouldn't lottery winners be a shining example of success? It takes striving for most of your life to earn what a lottery winner gets in one day. Sadly, some people just get to ruin their life more quickly. There has to be a better way.

I still had the same attitude about the lottery as I did about life. I'm a good person. God knows that if I win the lottery I would do good things with that money. I wouldn't ruin my life or the life of others, like all these other people do. I was extremely self-righteous. One night I had a dream that God was giving me the winning numbers in the lottery. I recall Him saying to me that He knows what numbers will be the winners tomorrow. I could still slightly remember the numbers He gave me when I woke up, but I didn't have a piece of paper near the bed and soon the numbers faded from my memory.

The next night I was better prepared. This might finally be it! I placed a pen and paper next to the bed. I knew that I would have the numbers I needed in the morning. I had another dream. This time God said to me, "I have the numbers you need." The numbers He gave me were 888. I wrote them down as soon as I woke up. I went to a grocery store later that day and bought a lottery ticket with those numbers on it. I knew there weren't enough numbers to win millions, but I thought God might be testing me. He might be making sure I would be diligent with the small winnings before He would give me the numbers for the big money.

I checked the numbers after the drawing. Needless to say, those numbers didn't win. I must have missed it. Maybe I wrote the numbers down wrong. Then I felt the Holy Spirit prompt me to check a small book on my shelf about the meaning of numbers in the Bible. The number eight means superabundance, resurrection and the beginning of a new era. I also searched around on the Internet and found that the number 888 is attached to Jesus. I had to laugh. I had been searching for an answer in this world, but God gave all of us something much greater than a winning lottery ticket. He gave us His precious Son. And in Him and through Him we have everything imaginable. We have that precious rest that the world is searching for. Our rest isn't a destination; it is a person. I keep that ticket in my journal as a reminder of the lottery I hoped to win, of the success I wanted in life, when everything I needed is found in His Son. All of us have the winning ticket available to us.

CHAPTER 4

There's Just One Problem

That last chapter was a little rough, I know. Don't worry, we are almost there. Let's keep moving. All of humanity has essentially the same problem. It may manifest itself in many different ways, but it shows up in everyone's life. The problem is that we live in a fallen world. Things are not getting better for us as a people or for the planet. When one disease is conquered, another more powerful one pops up. Hurricanes and earthquakes seem to be an almost daily occurrence across the globe. Things, in many ways, are getting worse day by day.

If you remember back to your Sunday school days you may recall the story of Adam and Eve, our original ancestors. In Genesis 1:26 God said, "Let us make man in our image, in our likeness…" and created them to rule over His creation. So they and we, their descendants, were made in God's image. We were also made to rule over creation. They, of course, had the benefit of being able to walk with God in the cool of the day. God described everything He made as good, but He described man as being very good.

That sounds like a pretty good start for us. Adam and Eve had a great relationship with our Creator. They lived forever. They had dominion over the entire planet. They had access to the mind of God. There was no disease, depression, poverty, hunger or natural disasters. There were none of the problems that mankind deals with today. So what happened?

What Happened in the Garden?

There were two trees specifically mentioned in the garden: the tree of life and the tree of the knowledge of good and evil. The tree of the knowledge of good and evil represents the law and self-effort. The tree of life represents Christ and God's grace. The tree of life was in the midst of the garden, but as with all of us, Adam and Eve looked to the tree that was off limits...the other tree. Both trees were part of creation, so they were both called good. The problem was that although it was good, the tree of the knowledge of good and evil was not good for man. It was off limits. Was it off limits to keep us in the dark and keep God's best from us? Absolutely not. God's best was the tree of life and it was always available.

The original humans were deceived by the serpent into believing God was holding out on them. Was God keeping His best from them? Nothing could have been further from the truth. They were made in God's image and had free access to Him. One of God's greatest gifts to us is our ability to choose. Adam and Eve would not have had a choice if nothing was off limits to them. They would also not have truly had a choice if all the available choices were good for them. So the tree of the knowledge of good and evil was placed off limits for our good. God wouldn't stop them from partaking of it, though.

After they ate of the fruit of the forbidden tree they brought a curse on themselves. This is what my pastor refers to as the "earth curse." The Bible says, "Cursed is the ground because of you; through painful toil you will eat of it all the days of your life. It will produce thorns and thistles for you, and you will eat the plants of the field. By the sweat of your brow you will eat your food..." (Gen. 3:17b-19). So the earth was cursed, but not by God's choosing. It was cursed by Adam and Eve's choosing. The rat race actually started long ago!

> The rat race actually started long ago!

God's natural state is giving and supply. Before the fall, His goodness flowed into Adam and Eve and into the world. It was a natural stream of goodness that they could partake of all the time. Blessing was natural in the world. After the fall, though, our ability to receive that stream of goodness dried up. From then on it was up to man to work for his success. He would strive for it on his own.

Up until this point, man had been led by his spirit. We are three parts: spirit, soul and body. Our soul took over when we fell. Our spirit went dark. Our spirit was the part directly connected to God. Our spirit had direct access to the love of our Father and to all His knowledge. Our soul is basically our mind, will and emotions. These are useful tools for the spirit to utilize, but they make extremely poor leaders in our life. We were left to try to learn all we could to survive. Earthly sense knowledge became extremely important. It was all we had. We started living from our soul instead of our spirit.

Looking for a Way Out

This curse applied to Adam and Eve and all of their offspring, which continues on with the human population to this day. Since that time humanity has struggled to survive. This is where our survival mentality comes from. It brings along with it an obsession with self. You become concerned with only yourself... "How will I survive? If I give to someone else, will there be enough for me?" It will show itself in two extremes. You either have a huge ego and think everything you achieve comes from the fact that you are awesome; or you feel you are a completely useless human of no value to anyone. As different as these two thoughts are, they are actually two extremes resulting from the same fallen world.

Overflowing Success

They both come from feelings of insecurity and inferiority. This results in lives filled with fear and worry for all individuals. We sit here alone on planet Earth, in the dark, as an orphan—missing the relationship we once had with our Creator. We exist to survive and end up fighting with each other as a result.

Today many people in the world try to improve their situation by going back to the original state of the garden. They eat only vegetables and simplify their lives to the bare essentials. There is nothing wrong with eating vegetables and there is definitely good to be had by simplifying your life, but it still misses the core problem of a fallen world. The vegetables you pick today are less nutritious than they were in the garden. Simplifying your life also overlooks the real issue of a fallen world. People can eat right, exercise, have a positive attitude and still end up with a horrible disease. These things do not make you immune from the earth curse.

By choosing the tree that was off limits Adam and Eve chose to give up their reign over the earth and handed it over to the enemy. They and their descendants would be slaves to that enemy and his system. People wonder why evil happens in the world. We can see why. Obviously God is not completely in control of the earth today. If He were, we would all be experiencing heaven on earth. Think of it as God owning the earth, but renting it to us. It's completely His, but we were left in charge. He gave that responsibility to us and we gave that responsibility away. I want to say all of this as reverently as possible. If God were in charge, then there would be no sickness, no natural disasters and no aging process. These problems come from the fallen world and the enemy. Man chose the wrong option for himself and for this world. Things in this world are breaking down. The rat race, disease, death—none of it comes from God. We were left in charge here, but we gave away our authority.

> We were left in charge here, but we gave away our authority.

As you can probably see, in the end we are all just searching for rest. This is the way out of survival mode. If we just had more than enough for our needs we could rest. If we can just win the lottery we can finally rest. If we become a billionaire then we can finally rest. If we just meet the spouse of our dreams we can finally rest. We are constantly on the search for that very elusive state of rest.

The good news is that we can finally rest. As believers we can live heaven on earth. The Israelites were released from slavery and eventually entered the promised land. God said they were entering His rest. Today we are released from our slavery of the earth curse and also enter into God's rest by one amazing gift: His Son, Christ Jesus.

CHAPTER 5

Our Success Has Already Been Provided

God's heart is to bless all of us with true success...His success. Success without any negative side effects. Overflowing success. The mistake we make under the "earth curse" is trying to achieve success by our own efforts. Created in God's image, we are all naturally designed to be successful. However, we find ourselves in this fallen world, whose natural state is failure. This is why we feel stuck.

Let's get to the really good news. It's even better than good news; it is the greatest news ever heard: Jesus already provided everything we need. I mean absolutely, positively everything we need. As He said at the cross, "It is finished." And it truly is. We are to rest in His finished work. This is the rest that brings true success. He has redeemed us from the earth curse mentioned in the previous chapter. He wore a crown of thorns to redeem us from the curse of painful toil. In fact, He has redeemed us from absolutely every curse that exists—disease, poverty, depression—all of it. As a believer in Jesus you have been born again. You are

Overflowing Success

a new creation and that new creation is not under the earth curse. You just choose to act like you are.

As believers in Christ we have access to the heavenly realm today. Our authority has been restored. We have direct access to God's Kingdom. As a result, we don't have to accept what this world is offering. In fact, we can pull the heavenly realm into the earth realm today. That's what Jesus did when He was on the earth and said we would do even greater things. When Jesus returns the world will be set right, but we can start setting things right in our lives today. We can help others to do the same. We don't have to wait. The Kingdom of God is in us right now!

Many are still living under the "earth curse" even though they are free. The cell door is unlocked but many sit there unwilling to leave. They are waiting for God to show up and hand them a check for a million dollars. Or they are waiting for the phone to ring with the job offer of a lifetime. Jesus has given us the keys to the Kingdom. We have been given the power to bring about the changes in our life that we need.

God gave us His Son; what else could we possibly need? Anything else we need in life is so much less than He already gave us. Why would He give us His Son and not provide health, success and great relationships? These are insignificant in relation to the gift of His Son. Of course they are provided! If we say they aren't then we are saying they are a greater blessing than His Son.

Many are also sitting back and waiting to go to heaven when they die. That's not truly living. The Bible says that when we receive Christ we receive "eternal life," not an afterlife. Eternal life is so much more than an afterlife. Don't miss out on all that Jesus has provided today. We need to step into the new life that Jesus paid for. New creations walk free of the earth curse right now—today!

When Jesus said He came to give us life, He was speaking to a crowd that was living and breathing. The word "life" here is translated from the Greek word zoe, which means the absolute fullness of life that belongs to God. It is real life, blessed and successful. It is abundant life. Jesus was actually putting God's life in us. That's why the Kingdom of God is in us. That's why the Holy Spirit resides in us. This world can't hold that back. With God's life in us, nothing can stand in our way!

> With God's life in us, nothing can stand in our way!

Like the Israelites in Egypt, we have been set free from our captivity. We are no longer slaves to the earth curse or our enemy. Also, like the Israelites, we will be tested in the desert. God will be with us, just as the Holy Spirit was with Jesus in the desert. We too have a land of rest already prepared for us. It is a land where we get to enjoy wonderful things that we did not produce. But, as with them, there are giants and those giants need to be handled. We do not need to be afraid; God has already given us the land.

When you pray, are you praying from a position that everything has already been provided or from one where God needs to do something additional for you? As I mentioned, most of us are waiting for God to do something. But Jesus provided everything on the cross. Everything. Again, Jesus cried, "It is finished." There is nothing left for God to do about your situation.

How to Make It Real

So why aren't you seeing this success in your life? It is because we have to pull God's finished work into this reality. We do this through our faith. Faith is simply believing God. This is still a fallen world and according to the Bible still under the control of the enemy. The enemy has been defeated by our Lord Jesus, we as His followers need to enforce that victory in the earth realm. We are to take dominion in our lives and help others take dominion in theirs.

The answers that come to us aren't going to be that magical check appearing in the mailbox. The answers are going to be creative ideas that God helps us walk out. The answers are going to be wisdom and favor with others. The answers are going to be supernatural healing for ourselves and for others. The answers are going to be divine appointments with people that will change our lives forever.

Jesus is the Lamb that took away the sin of the world. Your first step is knowing that your sin has been taken away by the blood of the Lamb. Sin consciousness keeps you from receiving the blessings that were paid for. You might be in a place where you hear about your sin each and every week. That price has already been paid. There is no need to discuss it further. I want to hear about Jesus and His finished work instead. Again, the price for our sin has been paid. In fact, it has been overpaid by the blood of Jesus. Hearing that good news is what gives us faith!

As I mentioned earlier, Joseph Prince talks about right believing leading to right living and I couldn't agree more. The more we talk about sin and the more we try to overcome sin in our own strength, the more sin there will be. Rest in Jesus' finished work. Jesus overcame sin itself. Sin was our nature, sin is no longer an issue for a believer who rests in Christ's finished work. It is no longer our nature. We are a new creation.

So not only is there great news that Jesus has taken away all of your sin, but also, according to the Bible, God remembers your sin no more. How amazing! God has chosen to forget it. It's not that sin went unpunished. Sin was fully punished at the cross. The word sin means missing the mark. Everything you have ever done or will ever do that has missed the mark has been removed. There is no need to discuss it again. If God chooses to forget it, who are we to keep bringing it up?

What freedom there is in this revelation! This allows you to relax and truly rest. It opens you up to receive the success that was paid for. Many today don't believe that people can handle this freedom. I assure you they can. Will they mess up? Absolutely, but nowhere near as much as they would being buried under a pile of guilt and condemnation. The things that used to draw me to a lower level of living no longer affect me. It's not that I have gritted my teeth and fought to overcome them in my life; that's self-righteousness. They are just not attractive to me anymore.

Our Success Has Already Been Provided

Don't waste the days of your life trying to overcome something that Jesus already paid for. We have something better, something greater than the appeal of all of the sin of the world combined. Rest in Him.

Our righteousness too is a gift—a gift from God. Thanks to Christ, we are now righteous before our heavenly Father. The problem with this revelation is that it takes away man's self-righteousness. It takes away the ability to say you deserve to be blessed because of your works or something you have done. When you see that others are resting in the finished work of Christ and being blessed while you are working so hard, you will say, "That's not fair," The truth is, it couldn't be more fair. We all have equal access to that rest.

The question is really this: what is your perception of God? Do you think He is a hard taskmaster or do you think He is your loving Father? Your answer to this question will take you down two different completely different paths.

If you think God is a hard taskmaster, you will be in constant fear of Him. You will be constantly looking over your shoulder. Are you working hard enough for Him? Did you read enough of your Bible today? Perfection is expected. You have to constantly look at yourself to make sure you measure up to the high standard set before you. This is the lifestyle attached to the law. It is man-focused.

If, on the other hand, you think God is your loving Father, you will come to Him in every situation. He becomes your answer. You run to Him instead of away from Him. One of the clearest times God ever spoke to me was when I was praying and calling Him Father. He told me to stop calling Him "Father"—He wanted me to call Him "Dad." Needless to say that stuck with me. It removed the walls of formality so present in the world today. Go ahead—try it if you haven't already. Call Him "Dad." Even in earthly relationships calling your dad, "father" seems so cold. It also makes our prayers seem cold. We should respect our dads, but there needs to be an intimacy there as the basis of the relationship. If there isn't, your standing is no different than that of an employee or a servant. The word used in the Bible for "Father" is Abba, which is even more intimate; it means Daddy. We should have no reservation in calling our loving heavenly Father, "Daddy."

In fact, this is the name for God that Jesus came to reveal. God has many names in the Old Testament and they are wonderful, but the most amazing name for our heavenly Father came through Jesus—we can call God, "Daddy." This is the lifestyle of grace. It is Christ-focused.

This may surprise some people, but God is in a great mood and He loves us beyond human understanding. You can't be in a better mood than God is. Sadly, few think of Him that way. He's not mad at you and He certainly isn't out to get you.

Dad Provides; Children Receive

Many of us focus on our limited ability to love God—and we should love Him. But real love is His love for us. Real love is His perfect love that casts out all fear. Your small child can never love you to the depth you love him or her. Your children can't give back to you in the same way you can provide for them. You wouldn't expect them to. You love being their provider. You love being their protector. In a way that is how God feels about us. He doesn't want us to look for satisfaction in the world. He wants us to come to Him for absolutely everything. He wants everyone to know that He takes good care of His children.

> God wants everyone to know that He takes good care of His children.

We also focus too often on the fact that all we have is God's... and it is. But let's remember that we are in covenant with Him. All that He has is ours! The lesser of the two in covenant always benefits the most in the relationship. That is always us. We benefit from God's limitless wealth, health and happiness. We are co-heirs with Christ. What Jesus now has, is what we now also have—everything in our Daddy's Kingdom.

Our Success Has Already Been Provided

Many prefer to pretend that we have a contract based on our performance. That contract doesn't exist. That's why you shouldn't be surprised when your paycheck doesn't come. Don't waste your time trying to perform to get in Daddy's favor. We are already blessed with His favor through Jesus.

One thing I find to be a big stumbling block for people is knowing how to receive from God. Just like the older brother in the prodigal son story, they think their life is task-oriented. They are working for Father while waiting for Him to bless us out of His choosing. As the father in the story said to that son, "All that I have is already yours." We have the inheritance; we have the entire estate already.

If it is already ours, why aren't we receiving it? I think part of the problem stems from the notion that it is better to give than to receive…and it is, from man to man, but not from God to man. From God to man we can only receive. After all, what can we give to God? God always takes the position of giver because He is the more blessed in our relationship. He is, in fact, the ultimate giver! He also has a multitude of angels to do His bidding. The things we might think we are giving to God are actually for our benefit. We must also remember that unless we first receive we will have nothing to give.

Please don't take this the wrong way, but Jesus came to be used. I heard Joseph Prince speak about this. I don't mean using Him as the people of the world use people. He came to be our savior, but we have to receive Him as our savior. We have to use Him as our savior. The Scripture says we have the mind of Christ; we are to use the mind of Christ. He is the Bread of Life—we are to consume Him. To not use and receive all He has provided is to just place God on a shelf. We are glad He is there, but He is not impacting our lives. Take from Him. Use Him. Receive from Him. He loves it! We receive it by our faith in Him. How sad it is that He has provided all and we shrink back thinking He doesn't want us to have it. That's an orphan spirit. A true son doesn't question his ability to receive within the family.

Jesus' power comes from knowing who He is. He is a Son. He is a King who serves. Jesus washed the disciples' feet. They would have had no trouble receiving this from a servant, but it's more difficult when it is God who wants to do that. It's human nature not to feel worthy of God's blessings. That's the "earth curse" talking. We must allow Him to bless us. Our power also comes from knowing who we are and whose we are; otherwise, all our effort is no different than that of a servant.

God called Jesus His Beloved before He did one miracle or changed one life on earth. He had been a carpenter, yet He was beloved by the Father. We too need to know who we are in Christ and know we are beloved before we do anything at all. Our success comes through knowing that before we step out in faith.

First, just relax and learn to receive from your heavenly Daddy. Rest in Him. He loves you and wants to provide for you. Obviously, He wants you to grow as a person, but that comes through your ability to receive from Him. Again, the lesser always receives from the greater. God does have one need that we can fill, though. It is to come home to Him as a son and have relationship with Him. A son may have chores, but that is not the basis of the relationship. The maid has chores too but at the end of the night she goes home. Regardless of the performance of the son, he remains a son. His desire to succeed is out of love for the family, not out of the duty of a servant.

Jesus never rebuked anyone for taking more from Him. He only rebuked them for taking too little from Him. Their "little" faith was about drawing too little on the limitless provision of God. He loves it when we trust in Him and draw from Him. When we take from Him it means we understand His goodness and His heart. He wants us to ask for bigger things in our lives. He loves it when we trust Him for things beyond our comprehension.

Jesus provided the way to restore our relationship with our Dad. How wonderful! The story of the prodigal son relates it perfectly. I highly suggest you pick up a copy of *The Birthright* by John Sheasby. John does an amazing job enlightening this parable.

In the story, a son asks for his inheritance before his father's death. According to the culture, this would be a real insult to a father of that day. The son then takes that inheritance and wastes it in a far-off land with rowdy living. When the money ran out so did the good times. The prodigal son eventually wises up and returns home hoping to be made a servant so he will have something to eat. The father sees him from a far distance (he has been looking for him) and runs to him (something fathers of that day would not do—it is undignified). He hugs him, kisses him and then does something amazing. He returns him to his rightful place of sonship—becoming a servant is not an option. Everything is restored to him. There was no begging, no pleading, no working as a servant until the father cooled off. There was none of that. He received the love and grace of the father right then and there.

In the same story the older brother is angry. A party is being thrown for the son who had returned. Why hadn't the older brother received a party all these years? He had behaved well and did what the father asked of him. That sounds like self-righteousness. As he put it, he "slaved" for the father. This is the lifestyle of the law. You expect to be rewarded for your performance. The younger son had squandered everything; why is he receiving a party? The father explains that all that he has, has been his older son's all along. In fact, the story indicates that the father divided the inheritance between both sons when the younger son left. So the older son had the entire estate available to him already, but he never drew on that inheritance. It's just the same with many believers today. All God has is ours and available, but we make no claim on it. We do not enjoy all that Jesus paid for. Our Dad's Kingdom is limitless. We can all take from Him for eternity and there is still much, much more.

We Are Sons!

Being a child of God is amazing! It starts out great and only gets better as you grow. One of your blessings is having the peace of Christ. So what if the entire universe collapses around you? You will still be standing with your loving Dad holding your hand. What peace! You also have been blessed with the mind of Christ.

Overflowing Success

Those who have the mind of the world think they have all the answers. With the mind of Christ you actually have access to all the real answers.

I mentioned before that after the fall we had to live from our soul realm. Thanks to Jesus we are now able to live from our spirit again. It is alive to God. Our spirit now finally rules over our soul and our body. It won't happen all at once. Your mind is used to being in charge. It won't give up control easily, but it has no choice. Our spirit is back and taking over. Start taking that territory today.

God so loved us that He sent what was most precious to Him, His Son, to redeem us or purchase our freedom out of the cursed world in which we live. How valuable are we to God? Priceless! How loved should we all feel? We have been brought out to rise above this world and to show others this same path to freedom and overflowing success.

As I mentioned before, Jesus also gave us His righteousness. This is critical for you to receive. Romans 5:17 says, "...those who receive abundance of grace and the gift of righteousness will reign in life through the One, Jesus Christ" (NKJV™). This is the key to reigning in life: receiving the abundance of God's grace and His gift of righteousness! Righteousness is a gift just like salvation. We can't earn it, so quit trying. When our Dad looks at us He sees Jesus and His righteousness. How can we not be happy with this revelation?

This is the key to reigning in life: receiving the abundance of God's grace and His gift of righteousness!

Also, there is no condemnation for those in Christ. Let's live like it! Condemnation is what is keeping so many of us in captivity. We are in Christ. That condemnation doesn't exist except in our minds. Jesus also conquered death. The fear of death is keeping many in the body of Christ in bondage. It is what mankind feared most, but it's been rendered powerless. How should we be living with this revelation? Much better and happier than we are.

Our Success Has Already Been Provided

What if every member of the body of Christ was living in the Kingdom of God and drawing on it daily? How different would our lives look? What kind of change can the body of Christ make in this world if we just got each member of the body completely debt-free? What could we do as a body if we got beyond paying our bills? What could the church do if all of our church buildings were paid off? How would the church grow if we paid our pastors what they deserve? How would we look to the world if we were all completely healthy and looked fifteen years younger than people our age? That all will happen when we start living up to our created potential. Change and influence take money in this world and in this system. Thankfully the Kingdom provides all we need for life and for our destiny.

How full would churches be if the world saw the answers to their problems inside our walls? The answers are there. The body of Christ needs to pull them from heaven into the earth realm and show the world all that Jesus has done. For example, Bill Johnson and his team at Bethel Church in Redding, California, are doing amazing things regarding physical healing. Go to their website at www.iBethel.org and see the wonderful healing testimonies. They are amazing! People have even received their healing through the internet. You can also watch the movies, *The Finger of God* and *The Father of Lights* by Darren Wilson. They feature Bethel Church and others that are impacting the world today. Your faith will be encouraged by the amazing things God is doing through His people today.

To be clear, I haven't reached the end of this path. I'm just getting started. I am learning as each of you are. As the Word says, we are being transformed into the image of His dear Son. It is in the knowing of both who you are and whose you are that you are transformed. You are redeemed from every curse through Christ. You have also received every blessing through Christ. You are in Christ, and you are a son or daughter of our heavenly Daddy. And that transformation changes not only your finances, your relationships and your life, but absolutely everything!

CHAPTER 6

Abundance of Love and Grace

The basis for everything in this book is God's abundant love and grace. I hope that shows. Love and grace are the power forces that flow out of God's Kingdom and into this world. They flow into our lives. They are the power that allows us to escape from the world's system. We are moved out of the kingdom of darkness and into the kingdom of light. This allows us to succeed by resting. We rest in Jesus' finished work on the cross. This results in overflowing success.

Most of us know what love is or think we do. Grace might be a little bit harder to define. Grace is God's freely given and completely unmerited blessing and favor. Grace is a gift. It is never earned. So you can't actually fall from grace by doing something wrong because it isn't earned in the first place. You can only choose to walk away from grace by trying to earn God's favor through your efforts.

The Father sent His Son because of His love for us and Jesus sacrificed Himself because of His love for us. Now we are only under His grace. Our life is no longer based on our performance, but on Jesus' performance. This is what allows us to thrive instead of just survive. It is how we receive and live a life of abundance, blessing, joy, health and peace.

My wife and I were able to pay off our mortgage through God's abundant love and His grace. We first had to be established in that love and grace to believe that it was possible. We stepped forward and walked out the steps needed on our end for the same reason. With each step, move forward a little more and constantly receive His grace. That's how you succeed. You have to believe you are loved unconditionally by our heavenly Father or you won't approach Him. You have to believe that He gives generously to His people or you won't ever ask Him for anything.

The alternative to this is self-righteousness and pay based on performance. Under this lifestyle you come up with the plan, then you work that plan for hours and hours each day. You sacrifice everything to reach your goal and hope that when you finally get there it was all worth it. By contrast, under grace, God gives you the plan and the plan is something you were created to do. It is something you love doing and in the end your life and the lives of others are better than than they were before. You reach your destiny and your success overflows.

His abundance of love and grace is what changes our hearts and actually brings us into His Kingdom. It is how we start taking dominion in our lives. It is how we start making the changes needed to create an amazing life. Too often we try to change ourselves and others in our own strength. We try to create our own success. If we do we are doomed to failure. If we do it through God's love for us and His wanting the best for us, it will be so much easier.

In mankind's beginning, God brought us into existence as someone He could love. We let go of that relationship, but God didn't let us go. He sacrificed that which was most precious to Him, His Son, to return us to right relationship with Him. That relationship is available to everyone, thanks to Jesus' sacrifice on the cross. God relentlessly pursues our hearts, wanting us to return home to Him.

As the Bible says, God is love. Love is not what He does; it is who He is. God's Kingdom is all about love. That's where the power comes from. You are able to enter His Kingdom when you believe that Jesus provided the access through His loving sacrifice on the cross. God loved us enough to sacrifice that which was most precious to Him to save us from our demise. Jesus loved us enough to pay the price for sin, death and every curse there is. Sin was overcome by the love of God, not the law of God. Jesus restored us to right standing with our heavenly Dad. We are now His sons and daughters. We have right standing in the family. We have access to all the blessings of God and He wants us to receive them.

Sin was overcome by the love of God, not the law of God.

It's the love of God that brings us to repentance. It's the goodness of God that leads people to repentance. Repentance means to change your mind. You change your mind about God. You return to Him. It's not the law or judgment of God that leads people to repentance. The law does what it was intended to do: it magnifies your need for a savior. You come to the end of yourself. Under law you follow the rules to perfection and then God blesses you. Under grace you receive God's goodness first and that leads to a change of heart, which also changes your actions. Jesus changed a tax collector's heart by loving him and spending time with him with no condemnation. The tax collector was guilty under the law. It was through Jesus' grace that the tax collector gladly overpaid the penalty for the fraud he committed.

Our Love Story

The entire Bible is God's love story about His Son Jesus. There are pictures of His beautiful Son throughout Scripture. You find them everywhere. Now that we are in Christ it is a love story about us also—the story of how much we were loved and the price that was paid to redeem us.

This understanding of grace makes many of the biblical accounts more understandable. Abraham believed God and was under His grace. Even when he lied, he was protected by the Lord. Under law his standing would be determined by his ability to keep the law. Abraham's relationship with the Lord began long before the law was given. The children of Israel were also under God's grace when they left Egypt. There was none feeble among them and they received wealth from the Egyptians. They all had their health and strength because they partook of the lamb at Passover. We too have health and strength available to us by the true Lamb and His stripes.

The children of Israel did not want a direct relationship with God, though. They preferred to relate to God through a man: Moses. As such, they said they were well able to do all that God would ask them to do. That's self-righteousness. They turned away from grace and the tree of life and wanted to be judged by their own performance and the tree of knowledge of good and evil. Their grumblings went unpunished under grace, but it was a different story under law.

God also judged the nation by their high priest. If the high priest was bad, the nation was bad. If the high priest was good, the nation was good regardless of their individual performance. Today Jesus is our high priest. We are in Christ and we are judged by His standing. His standing is perfect. The priest also did not judge the person who brought a sacrifice; the priest judged the lamb that the person brought. The priest didn't look at the person, only the lamb. If the lamb was accepted, the person was accepted. Our Lamb is beyond perfect. Anytime you feel condemned or accused, point to your perfect sacrifice on the cross: our Lord.

As I said before, the law was written for man to come to the end of himself and to know that he needed a savior. Jesus fulfilled the law perfectly on our behalf. And although the law is inflexible, the basis of the law is love. For example, if you love someone, you won't steal from that person. The problem is that it is our love. It rests on us and our strength to make it happen. Jesus said to love the Lord your God with all your heart and with all your soul and with all your strength and with all your mind. This was in response to a question about the law. The law depends on us to fulfill it. It brings us to despair by making us look at ourselves.

A Higher Truth

There is a higher truth and it is this: we love because He first loved us. This is grace. Grace is dependent on God, not us. Grace is higher than law. We can love our neighbor because we know God loves us. When you receive His love you have no choice but to overflow that love toward others.

Our earthly version of love is really a love of self. You love someone else for what he or she can do for you. You love that person for the beauty, finances or entertainment he or she can provide you. Many of our most popular books, television shows and movies emphasize that.

The truth is that love is sacrifice. God so loved the world that He gave His Son. Jesus gave Himself willingly for us. Love gives. God gives beyond human understanding. There is a real price to love others. The good news is that we can receive love from the original source: God Himself.

The best thing you can do with God's love is receive it. Soak up all the love you can handle. Fill up on all you can take until you overflow with the love of God. Then let that overflow spill into the lives of others. When you are filled to capacity and overflowing you are in position to change your life and the lives of others. Success comes when you base everything you say, think and do on love. This is truly overflowing success.

> Success comes when you base everything you say, think and do on love.

Nobody wants you coming to him or her on the street and declaring that you have good news. People do not want to hear that one day, when they leave this world, they can finally have success and happiness. Until then, they are just to survive and get by. Also, don't say, "Here is a list of rules to follow, which you won't be able to follow perfectly." Nobody wants that news. That news doesn't change lives.

You are instead the long-lost brother or sister who returns to the orphans in the street to tell them the good news: Our Father wants them all to come home. It was not the Father who was lost but the orphans. He has more love, more health and more abundance than they will need both today and throughout eternity. He will heal all the wounds they have from the world and its system. He is ready for all of them to come home today!

Love overcomes the barriers to success in our lives. Fear is what holds us back. Perfect love casts out all fear. That perfect love is our Father's love. You first need to sit under God's love for a while. Many of us coming from the world's system into the Kingdom of God need some time to just be loved. Don't be in a hurry. Soak in that love as long as it takes.

CHAPTER 7

A Change of Heart

What happens when you soak in God's love? Your heart becomes softened and changed. This is the change that is needed to really put your life in order and be open to success. It is a heart change. When I got to the place where our mortgage was paid off and where amazing things were happening in our lives on a regular basis I looked back and realized that the real change came in my heart. The change wasn't immediate but came over time. When your heart changes, you change. If your heart doesn't change and only your behavior or actions change, it won't last. You'll find that God is interested in transforming your heart. He's not interested in changing your behavior.

Change in Perception

The first change is in your perception of God. This is what I covered in a previous chapter. You see God as your loving Daddy and see Jesus as saving you in every way possible. He provided something you couldn't provide for yourself through good behavior or your own efforts. So rest and relax. Enjoy your new position and the success that comes with it.

When you begin with this as your starting point, the Bible comes alive. You start to rightly divide the Bible by seeing Jesus relating differently to the those who came to Him by the law and their works (the rich young ruler) and those who came to Him by His grace (the tax collectors and the prostitutes). The rich young ruler was concerned with his performance and didn't see that he had actually placed money before God. So he had in fact broken the law he thought he kept. The tax collectors and prostitutes made no attempt to pretend they had kept the law. They knew that they could only rely on grace. The same is true today. Do you expect to receive because of your good behavior or do you expect to receive because of God's grace?

You will also begin to understand that Jesus said some things in the Bible before He paid the price on the cross and some things after. That's why I like Paul's letters as a starting point in the Bible. Starting with Paul's revelation of grace opens up the rest of the Scripture.

I wasted too many of my early years in self-righteousness. I went to church each week and learned what was wrong and what not to do and I followed the rules. I would bend them a bit when I didn't do something just right. Then when things didn't go my way I would get angry. After all, I was doing my part. Like the older brother in the prodigal son story I was expecting my reward, but it never came.

What changed? In essence I sought first the Kingdom of God and His righteousness and all these things were added to me. I realized that my righteousness comes through Christ. Again, it is a gift. It can't come through me. I was wasting my time trying. Many people think seeking first the Kingdom means doing more for God, such as going to church more often, praying more or volunteering at the church more. However, His Kingdom is already in us. We are already the righteousness of God in Christ. We aren't trying to gain righteousness. We already have it through Christ.

It does mean putting God first in your life—just not in the way most people think. God loves you more than anyone ever will and

A Change of Heart

He wants your life to be better than even you want it to be. On top of that He is the most powerful being there is, and even better than that He is your Dad. If He counts the number of hairs on your head, He cares about even the smallest detail of your life. You put Him first in your life because nobody cares more about you than God does. Nobody wants the best for you more than God does. Nobody is able to do more for you in your life than God can. To have anything else in your life before Him is just silly.

Nobody cares more about you than God does.

When you and your spouse put God first in your marriage, your communication with each other opens up. Your relationship can only get better. You both are actually having a relationship through Him. It's not in your own strength. You can both rest because you aren't trying to "win" in the relationship.

When you put your spouse or your children first in your life it is a recipe for disaster. No matter how wonderful a spouse or how great a child you have, he or she doesn't do very well in first place in your life. Even though your intentions may be good and it may make sense in the natural, it is a recipe for disaster in the spiritual.

That being said, after God, your spouse needs to come next in your life. Your children must come third. I always had a problem with this. I saw children as helpless and needing our attention more than our spouse does. The truth is the best thing we can do for our children is model a healthy, God-centered marriage for them. Nothing will provide them with more comfort or direction. If your children see that they take center stage ahead of your spouse, they will leverage that position for their own gain. As we discussed before, this is a fallen world and even our adorable children will play the game to win.

As you hopefully have come to realize, our relationship with God is as a son (both for the male and female among us). By this I mean we have the position of son. We have everything that comes with being part of the family. We get to participate in family kingdom business. We have all the rights and benefits of a son of the

King. We need to step into them. Everyone wants to know where they stand in the family. Let me assure you, you belong and you are unique. Our family needs you!

Change in Trust and Integrity

Another one of the initial heart changes is trust. We have all been burned by the world's system and by our earthly friends and families. We translate this into our relationship with God. Let me assure you that God is not out to trick you. He is unable to do that. The Bible says God is unable to lie. Every promise in His Word is true. His love for you is never-ending and unable to be measured. Do not warp His perfect unconditional love by your view of love in this fallen world. He is the only one you can place one hundred percent of your trust in.

As I also mentioned before, we are being transformed into the image of Jesus. He is the perfect Son of our Father. Jesus is also the perfect example of the Father. Jesus said if you had seen Him, you had seen the Father. Our Father in heaven is young and vibrant like Jesus. No one is old in heaven. He's also in a great mood, as I mentioned before. Many of us don't act like He is. So as we are transformed, we are renewing our youth and becoming full of life. Just like Dad, we should also be in a good mood. Many other things about us will also change. We will start to be more trustworthy, for example, just as Jesus and our Father are. When we say we will do something, we mean it. It's not through our effort but through our new nature. People will see Christ in us.

Our Father in heaven is young and vibrant like Jesus.

This transformation comes in part through our integrity. This is definitely an area you will be tested in—usually in the small things. Someone will give you more change back than you had coming at the drive-thru. Someone will neglect to charge you for your drinks at a restaurant. Making sure you correct these little inaccuracies will go a long way in shaping your character and

A Change of Heart

integrity. Many would say, "Hey, I get ripped off all the time. This is just a little payback." But trust me, acting with integrity in all things will change your life.

Make sure you do everything in your life with integrity. You represent Christ on earth; you are an ambassador. People are watching to see if you are really different than everyone else. I'm not perfect at it, but I'm miles away from where I once was. At the same time, don't make it a law in your life. Do it out of love and do it out of your position. The child of the King doesn't need to sneak an extra dollar from a fast food restaurant. Like I said, it's not a law to be followed; rather, it is a demonstration of your new nature.

God is also an extreme giver and not a taker as many think of Him. The heart change you will experience will also make you more of a giver. When you realize your Dad has unlimited wealth and unlimited time you start to loosen your grip on those things in your life. Giving a few extra minutes to a co-worker going through a rough time does not take away time you need to succeed. Your success comes through rest, which is a result of your position, not of striving like those in the world. That is the type of success that overflows. You can freely give to your church and those in need because you know your heavenly Dad will take care of you. Your transformed heart and the leading of the Holy Spirit will show you where to invest that time and money.

A major part of the heart change is to start looking at Jesus and away from yourself. The more you look at yourself the worse you will feel. Many advise looking inward. I suggest the opposite. Look away from yourself and look at Jesus. The more you look at Jesus, the better you will feel. You will see the amazing things that He has done for all of us. You will see the position He has restored to us. You will see your value in what God gave up to save you—He gave up His perfect and precious Son to redeem you. How amazingly valuable are you to God!

Once you begin to receive this revelation and the blessings of God, then let them flow freely out of you. The source of that success is limitless. Out of your belly will flow rivers of living water. Let it flow to your friends, neighbors and even your enemies.

Bless all who do you wrong. You are no longer of the world; you are a child of God who does not need to hold a grudge. Those who stand against you cannot withstand the river of God's love flowing out of you.

The main family responsibility for all of us is to share this good news with the rest of the world. The best way to share is by letting everyone see the success in your life from God's Kingdom. They will want to know how it happened. There is unlimited space at our Father's house. Share the blessings you experience with others and let them know those blessings are freely available to them also.

One important last point here. We do not to clean ourselves up to come home to God. That's backwards. We are to come to God damaged and dirty from the world and receive all that Jesus has paid for. We are washed clean by the blood of the Lamb. To say there is something someone must do on top of that is to insult the sacrifice of Jesus. Also, know that God has chosen you. He has a wonderful plan for your life and He will help you reach your destiny. If you are reading this book and have not returned home to Daddy, simply put this book down and, out loud, ask Jesus to come into your heart right now. Come home. As simple as that sounds, it will change your universe. You'll never regret it and it will start you on an amazing adventure.

CHAPTER 8

Your Vision

Now that your heart is changed, what happens next? You need to ask yourself a few questions. What has God shown you as the direction for your life? What is it you want to accomplish? What has been placed in your heart? What is it you want to change in your life? Is it to be completely debt-free and to pay off your mortgage? It could be anything. Is it to have a better relationship with someone in your life? Is it to work in an occupation in which you find fulfillment? Is it to enjoy a healthier body?

The question is really this: what portion of what you do in your life right now is significant? In other words, what are you doing that has real value? Up until now you have just been thinking of survival—putting food on the table, having clothes to wear, etc. Now that you are free of the kingdom of darkness, you don't need to chase after these things. Things and money are there to serve you as a child of the King. So what things of significance do you want to achieve?

Regardless of your answers, you will need a vision for those things you want to achieve. Your desire needs to be for something so big that you know you won't be able to do it in your own strength. A real plus to this is that you will be wise enough not to even try it in your own strength. It should make you uneasy. Some people would say it should make you scared, but how can you be scared when you know God is with you? Regardless, it should stretch you. It should stretch your faith. It should stretch your life. How does your life have to change in order to become the person you want to be?

For example, let's say you wanted to pay off your mortgage in five years. Most people right away are going to say that is impossible. They have eliminated their success before they even start. By our story in Chapter 1 you know that it is possible. We did it. It wasn't easy and we didn't do it without God, but it is completely possible. So the first step is to eliminate impossibility from your mind and especially from the words you speak. As a child of God all things are possible to those who believe.

Try to approach everything with a childlike faith in God. Regardless of the vision, the idea or the mountain in the way, first remember that there is absolutely nothing that can stop God. And if He is for you, nothing can stop you. Too often I think we tend to over think everything. That is living from our soul. We filter everything through our past experiences, our knowledge of what has happened to others or our education. We need to let all that go and focus on the One who has the power to change everything in our life in a split second. Many times those who have the most education regarding a certain area of life have the most trouble receiving from the Kingdom in that area.

Two Questions

The first question most Christians have is whether or not what they want for their life is God's will. Let's return for a minute to remember who God is. He is our loving Father and our biggest fan. He is our Daddy. Would your perfect Daddy want you out of debt? Would He want you completely healthy? Would He want you to have a life that is free from the stress and bondage of the world? Of course He would! He also wants to help you along the way. He wants you to grow and to succeed. He wants to work with you to make that happen. God is the God of success!

God's will is defined for us by the Lord's prayer. In it Jesus said His will is to be done on earth as it is in heaven. Heaven is a place where God's will is done constantly. Obviously this world is not heaven, but we have His Kingdom in us. So His will is that our lives reflect heaven. We should be enjoying heaven on earth. Jesus demonstrated this when He walked the earth. We should be debt-free, we should have amazing relationships and we should find joy in our daily endeavors. We should be completely healthy, happy and full of life. Our lives should be so amazingly different that people make a point to ask us what's going on. They see the remarkable fruit in our lives.

> Our lives should be so amazingly different that people make a point to ask us what's going on.

I recently read a book called *Walking in the Will of God* by Steve McVey. It covers this topic extremely well and would be a good option for those looking to learn more about God's will for their lives.

A second question will probably pop up. Why doesn't God just snap His fingers and make our life instantly change? He doesn't do that for the same reason lottery winners almost always end up in worse shape than they began. It is also for the same reason parents who pay off their son or daughter's debt find that child back in debt in a few years. Giving someone what he or she wants or even needs does not solve the underlying issue. This is not to say that God doesn't save people from situations; He absolutely does. He is our Savior after all.

The underlying issue starts with the change of heart mentioned in the previous chapter. Once you have the change of heart you can begin changing the circumstances in your life. If you don't have a heart change first you would be hurt, not helped, by receiving what you are asking for. God's chosen people, the Israelites, cried out to Him during their slavery in

Egypt. He freed them from their bondage just like you have been freed from the bondage of the earth curse. But God did not snap His fingers and have them immediately occupy the cities of the promised land. They needed to get the slavery mentality out of their thinking. They needed to grow, change and take dominion for themselves...just like we need to do. But best of all, God is with us through it all.

Exploring Your Vision

So what do you see for your family? We already mentioned being out of debt—including your mortgage—and I think that is a great goal for all families. It gives you the ability to have peace in your relationships. It helps you to sleep better at night. It gives you options in your career. Best of all, it frees you up to give back to the Kingdom of God. This includes your financial giving, the giving of your time and your ability to help others. This is definitely an important area of overflowing success. I would never have been able to sit down and write this book without removing the pressure of debt and the earth curse from my life. Thanks to Jesus and His sacrifice I am able to do something that I enjoy and that brings value to others.

You'll discover that your vision will not be about the pleasures of life. Those are provided by God when you seek first His Kingdom. God wants you to enjoy life. He wants you to have things and activities that you enjoy. You will find, though, that if you seek first the pleasures you will never truly receive them. You'll also never end up enjoying the pleasures you think you have received. So a goal of early retirement and lying on a beach is not a vision for your life.

Your vision will likely involve helping others or helping you to be able to help others. A vision of becoming debt-free does so many things. It shows your children the importance of being debt-free. It shows your friends, neighbors and relatives that it can be done. It also allows you to help others and to speak into their lives when they have a need. We see success overflowing

Your Vision

again. You get to share what God is doing in your life. People still bring up our paid-off home mortgage years later to us and tell us how inspiring it is to them.

Remember, nothing is impossible with God. Our vision another year was to have a beautiful and healthy baby boy. Your vision can be anything. It can be having children, sending a child to college, starting an orphanage, starting a business. The options are limitless; use your heart and the direction of the Holy Spirit to show you the way.

Make your vision just beyond your reach. If you can do it without God, it's not a vision for your life; it's just a task. This shouldn't just be an accomplishment but a life-changer. What change in your life would make your life shine brighter? What change would allow you to share what God has done in your life? What change would prompt people to ask you how you did it?

You need to actually see the place you want to reach. We had to see ourselves as parents of a beautiful and healthy baby boy. We had to see ourselves living in a paid-off home. Picture it in your mind and especially in your spirit. We sought out others who had also become pregnant after struggling to conceive. We also sought out debt-free stories. We needed to hear that other people were achieving what we were reaching for. Whatever it is you want to accomplish, you must be able to see it. Find others who have done it and hear their stories. Read articles about people who have done it. Watch videos to encourage you. See yourself in the delivery room. Take a tour of the maternity wing. See yourself mailing in that final credit card payment. See yourself walking into the mortgage company and paying off your mortgage. Actually drive to the building that holds your mortgage and walk around. Go up to the teller and ask what you would need to do to pay off your mortgage, even if it is only day one of your new vision. Learn the process, see the sights and smell the smells. Make it real.

We walked into the bank and asked what the process was before we ever paid off our mortgage. That really helped to make our vision real. When we returned to the bank in December of 2009 to pay off our mortgage we asked them to take our picture.

Overflowing Success

Don't be shy. Whatever your vision is, enjoy every moment of the journey. We make sure that we savor every moment with our beautiful son. He is such a blessing in our lives! These are big events in your life—relish them!

Remember to keep a record of all the amazing blessings God is providing in your life. If you are just starting out, start with a list of everything He has already provided. Your health, your family, your country, your education, your career, your talents. Don't ever think you are a completely self-made success. The blessings of God and others in your life have brought you to this place. Thankfulness is a key to overflowing success. Being thankful for the things that you may have overlooked opens you up to receive more blessings.

Thankfulness is a key to overflowing success.

Remember that as soon as you have made your request known to God it is already finished in the spiritual realm. You've asked something according to His will and now it is yours. It may not have arrived yet in physical form, but it is on its way. You are taking steps from this point forward knowing that it is already yours and you are acting on that knowledge.

One thing I know for sure is that husbands and wives need to be on the same page no matter what the vision is. You must be in agreement. Your vision has to be the top priority for both of you. My wife and I would look at each other often and say, "What's our top priority? Having a baby." Or when a tempting way to spend money would come along we would need to be able to look each other in the eye and say, "What's our vision? What's our priority here?" As with any journey you need to agree on the destination before you start heading down the road. You know there will be bumps and turns along the way. When you start off in agreement, it makes those things so much easier to overcome.

Be sure to write your vision down. Put it in a place you can return to and see it. Some people like to put it on their refrigerator. We did. Some like to put it up in their bathroom, to see it every morning before work. Do whatever you like to keep that vision in front of you. Keep it in your planner. Place it in your wallet. Make it a commitment. Both of you need to be in agreement that you want to receive your vision.

Now that you have your vision, it is time to start preparing for success.

CHAPTER 9

Preparing for Success

Let's start preparing for your success. Your vision is the picture of where you want to end up. Now it is time to plan the trip itself. Keep in mind that your plan is just that—a plan. Odds are, the actual path you take to get to your destination will be completely different. The plan just gets you moving and helps you head in the right direction. Your vision is what propels you though. If something comes along that will help you to reach your vision but is not in your plan, and you feel the Holy Spirit is directing you to do it, by all means do it.

Your success has already been achieved in Christ. What we are talking about by planning is not a matter of striving and strategizing the world's way. Rather, it is moving forward out of a state of rest in Christ's finished work. We know that our efforts alone amount to nothing. But when we step forward in faith, believing that our success is already ensured, we can relax and enjoy the journey.

So relax and talk to God about your vision and your plan to achieve it. Have a conversation with Him. Rest and share your heart with Him. He created you. He placed that vision you have in your heart. God is your perfect heavenly Dad. You can trust Him. Talk to Him about the vision and the plan you have. Be sure to do this before you start heading toward your vision and throughout the journey. If you are off track, He can bring you back to the correct path. Praying constantly just means throughout the day. It's not a work. Take a moment here and there to talk to Dad about everything going on in your life, not just your vision. It could be about absolutely anything. He is there for you!

These steps are making room for the delivery of what you are believing God for. You are making room in your life for the arrival of your weight loss, the arrival of your new baby, the arrival of your new job. Your life, as it is now, does not have room to contain what you have a vision for. It has to change to make room for it.

Clean Out and Write Down

One of the first things you might do in the planning stage is clear out the clutter from your life. This makes room for the overflowing success that is coming. It makes it easier to receive. Clean out the basement, your closets, even under the kitchen sink. It is simple to do and really makes you feel like you are moving in the right direction. After all, your possessions are not you. Many times people hold on to things out of fear. All that clutter is not your life. You are a spiritual being living a physical life. Don't get bogged down by adding pounds and pounds of possessions to your life. Knowing your Dad's perfect love for you should be casting that fear out. You have eternity to spend with your loved ones. Am I saying get rid of all your sentimental items? Definitely not, but you do need to make a decision. Are you moving forward to the new you or are hanging on to the old you? Are you hanging on to your old life or grabbing hold of your new life?

Will cleaning things out get you to your vision? No, but it's all about moving in the right direction. I would guess that most people who reach their vision are rather organized and not burdened with piles of stuff. People who have a lot of clutter in their home also seem to have clutter in the rest of their life. So start working on cleaning out the clutter. Don't make it overwhelming or you won't do it. Just tell yourself you will clean out a box a week. Increase the amount as you get rolling. Maybe start with your basement, then move on to your closets. Get rid of those items in your closet that still have tags on them and have never been worn.

> It's all about moving in the right direction.

Giving is a key to overflowing success. Give away all of the items you have cleaned out of your house. Give them to people in need. Give them to friends and family. You will start to feel more free. You will start to be able to think more clearly. You will start hearing more clearly what God is speaking.

Now that you have the clutter cleared out of your life it should be easier to write down your plan. Write out the smaller, individual goals that get you to your future vision. What steps need to be accomplished on the way to your vision? What are your priorities? Making sure your children and spouse are provided for should be at the top. Make sure you are covered in the area of insurance for your family. This should be one of your first goals. Also, be sure to have a will in place. Get the basics of life covered before you step out in faith.

You will probably have several things in your plan that aren't fun to do. Let's use my paid-off mortgage again as an example. My wife and I had to track our spending. We needed to see what we were spending and where we were spending it. Our biggest surprise was in the area of food. We were spending an extraordinary amount on groceries and dining out. When we saw where the leaks were we could take action to plug them. If you remain in the dark, the problem never gets solved.

Think Long-Term

Regardless of your present vision, you should also have a long-term plan for your life. Most people just muddle through life

Overflowing Success

in reaction mode. They are in a constant state of reacting to problems. Many problems are not a surprise. Have an emergency fund in place for problems. Cars are going to need repairs; roofs are going to need replaced. Be ready for it. Many people live their life too close to the edge of the cliff. If one little thing doesn't go their way, they get pushed off that edge.

I remember when we first thought about long-term planning with cars. We had never considered it before, but we all know we will need new transportation in the future. So what do we all do? We go to the dealership and see what kind of payment we can afford. This is crazy! We added cars to our long-term planning. We estimated when we would need a new car and how much we would need to save in order to pay cash for our next car. This is probably another moment where you are saying, "That is impossible!" Believe me, it's not impossible. If we didn't take the next step of buying a car with cash, how could we expect to pay off our mortgage? Remember, God will help you. Don't think of all this as a burden on your shoulders. Your new state of being is rest. What this did was change our thinking about cars. Maybe we can get by with a used car instead of a new one. Maybe we can do just as well with a $15,000 car as we can with a $30,000 car. When we visualize having to hand over cash for such a large purchase it changes the whole equation.

The idea of delaying gratification helped us along the way to becoming debt-free. Maybe we didn't need the newest phones and computers when they came out. Perhaps we can wait a year or two until they are half the current price and the kinks are worked out. Maybe we don't need them at all and our current one will do just fine. Such planning changes your thinking. We just ordered bedroom dressers this week. We haven't had them in our entire marriage. We could have bought them a long time ago, but when you become a long-term purchaser, you really think before you make a purchase.

The simple solution was to just pay cash for everything we buy, all the way up to cars. If we don't have the cash we don't buy it. It is logical if you think about it. If you don't have the cash then you are borrowing someone else's cash (via a credit card, etc.) to purchase an item that could end up costing you double the original purchase price before you are done. Is it any wonder people aren't getting ahead?

The simple solution was to just pay cash for everything.

Just like the credit card example, you end up paying roughly double the price of your house (depending on the interest rate) if you take the entire thirty years to pay it off. A $200,000 house ends up costing you around $400,000. Will it be worth $400,000? Probably not in today's real estate market. What could you do with that extra $200,000 you are going to pay the bank? I'm sure you have better use for it.

These are just examples of things we did. In the same way, take your vision and break it down into steps. Break those steps down into smaller, more manageable steps. Write down what needs to change in you to reach your vision. What are you doing today that you need to stop doing? What aren't you doing today that you need to start doing? Again, you are just setting up the basic steps, not drawing up a professional business plan.

As you did with your vision, write down your plan. I mentioned this is just the outline to get you moving, but it also needs to be concrete and available to review and change as needed. Write out the steps you need to reach your vision. For our mortgage, it was to first pay off all our consumer debt. Next, we wanted to pay cash for cars. As we kept paying off each debt, we would roll the money we freed up into an extra payment on our mortgage. We also made sure we were receiving direction from God along the way.

I hope this chapter showed the power of being proactive rather than reactive. I also hope it showed the power of long-term planning for your life. Prepare for the success and the blessing that is coming. Have a plan and start heading toward your vision. In the next chapter, we take being proactive a step further as we start to take dominion in our lives.

CHAPTER 10

Taking Dominion in Your Life

As I mentioned in a previous chapter, God sets you free but you need to take territory just like the children of Israel did. This chapter is about taking dominion in your life. There are many areas you probably need to take dominion over. These are the areas in your life that currently don't reflect heaven. It could be your finances, your job, your relationships or your health. You will know when there is something in your life that you need to take dominion over. God will help you.

When you believe in something, you take action. When you believe the things you say you take action in their direction. If you believe God will bless you with a better car, then you start cleaning out the garage. Just like when you believe guests are coming over for a visit, you start preparing the house. The same is true in our lives. When you believe something, you take action. When we were believing God for our baby boy, we started getting his room ready. We were expectant. In the heavenly realm our son was already on his way, so we needed to prepare just as we discussed in the previous chapter.

Overflowing Success

Dominion is the next step in that process. When you are taking dominion in an area of your life you are taking that area out of the world's system and placing it under God's Kingdom. When Jesus blessed the loaves and fishes He placed them under His Dad's Kingdom and they multiplied. He took them out of this world's system and supernaturally multiplied them by placing them under God's Kingdom.

Let's take another example. Suppose you want to take dominion in your health. You start by placing your health and everything connected to it under God's Kingdom. You take it out of your hands and put it into His hands. You notice that you currently only eat cupcakes at each meal. You feel that cupcakes for every meal is not helping your health, so God helps you to eliminate them. He limits your sugar cravings. At this point you still haven't taken dominion. Dominion is replacing the cupcakes with something much better. Let's say you replace the cupcakes with a well-balanced meal. You have placed your eating desires under God's Kingdom. Whole foods start tasting better to you. Eating those well-balanced meals starts making you feel better physically. Since you feel better, you start walking more. This makes you feel even better. Eventually you feel good enough to start working out. God blesses the workouts and you tone up faster than expected. You start really getting into shape. People begin asking how you are doing it. You get to share God's Kingdom with others and you start helping others get in shape. Now working out is a pleasure and it takes a lot less effort to maintain your new body. Eventually you have created a place of perpetual success where anarchy and disorder once reigned. You have removed that area of your life from the world's system and placed it under the Kingdom's system. It started in the spiritual realm and now you see it's manifestation in the physical realm. You have taken dominion over that area of your life. However, you and I must make sure we are not following this process from our own strength. When you put them under God's authority, you'll find that God takes the areas of your greatest weakness and failure and turns them into glorious success stories.

God takes the areas of your greatest weakness and failure and turns them into glorious success stories.

By taking dominion, you are enforcing the finished work of Christ in the earth. Since you have been given the role of ambassador of God's Kingdom, you have the authority. You can take dominion wherever you have authority. This can be in your life, your children's lives, your body, your home or your business. You can't take dominion in someone else's life, but you can show another how he or she can do it for him or herself.

Guard Your Words

The first area to take dominion over is one of the most important: your words. Take control of all of the words that come out of your mouth. Take control of the words you say on the computer. God created the entire universe with His words and we are made in His image. That means when you believe something in your heart and you speak it with your mouth, it comes to pass. We are a member of the royal family and the decrees of royalty have power. Our words have the power to create or destroy in our life. The Bible says life and death are in the power of the tongue. When my wife and I became aware of this, we started to see the impact people's words were having in their life. How often do people predict failure in their life, only to see it come to pass? Pay attention to what others are saying and the results they are seeing in their lives. Even simple little expressions that are common are so negative.

Choose your words very carefully. We make sure we do. Start speaking or planting positive words in your life and in the lives of others. Speak only words of success and achievement. You'll see the results of those words appear in your life very soon.

A great way to start take dominion with your words is to encourage others. It is one of the best ways to use the words that come out of your mouth. You may be the only person living in the Kingdom of God whom someone may see in his or her life. Speak love. Speak words of encouragement to people. Be a blessing in their lives. Like a dry field, your words of encouragement will be soaked up by the thirsty recipients of the world.

You can use your words to take dominion in many situations. Use your words to speak to your body when you feel ill. Command your body to be well and the illness or problem to be gone in Jesus' name. Disease has zero right to be in your body when the Kingdom of God is in you. Jesus gave us the authority to use His name. As believers we are resting in His finished work. Bind the illness and loose healing and health in your body. Speak words of healing directly to your body. Speak to the area needing healing. Don't give weight to the words anyone else says about your health; give weight to the words of your Savior!

Allow God to work in your life. Don't block Him from working in your life by thinking that you have to solve everything on your own. Let Him be God in your life. Relax, smile and laugh—your success is not based on your effort, but His.

You can also speak to your finances. Say out loud that your credit card is paid off. Speak to your house—say out loud that your house is paid off. It may not be paid off in the natural, but you can speak it into the spiritual realm. Tell your body that your weight is so many pounds fewer than it is in the natural. The natural realm will have to line up with your words. Again, you are made in God's image and redeemed back into correct relationship with your Father. His words have power and so do yours.

My wife and I use our words to thank Jesus all day long. We thank Him out loud for everything. If we need a good parking spot, we thank Him for it before we get there. If we need good weather for an outing, we thank Him for it before the outing. We can thank Him before all of these things because we know He loves us and wants the best for us. Most of the time we get what we thank Him for, or even something better. If it doesn't go the way we wanted or hoped, we don't worry about it. We are at rest. All things are working together for our good, regardless of how it looks. It just means something better is on the way.

Guard Your Heart

As I said before, this all starts with a change of heart. According to His Word we are to guard our heart above all things. We do this by guarding what we allow to enter our eyes and our ears. What are you reading, what are you watching, what are you listening to? Too often we watch and listen to the same things as the people of the world and then wonder why our lives look identical to theirs.

Take dominion over what you put into your mind. Your mind is very fertile soil. Obviously the television shows we watch have a big impact on the results of our life. What we take in every day has a great impact on what we produce every day. If it's not adding to your life, eliminate it.

One of the best things I ever did was stop watching local and national news. Do you really need to hear about the fears and concerns of the media? If there is something you need to hear about, trust me, somebody will be talking about it. When it comes to national news, how much of it is based on the fear of things that probably won't even happen? I hate to break it to you, but most of the time they don't happen. Save yourself the stress and check the headlines on a news website for one minute twice a day. That will keep you informed enough and save you an hour that you can use more productively. The idea is that when you change yourself and help others to change themselves, there will be less and less of this bad news to report anyway.

Don't waste your time spending hours watching and worrying about the world. Worry does zero for us and for others. Spend those hours improving yourself instead and helping others to do the same. Obviously, pray about situations that concern you. We need to pray that His will be done in the earth realm. If we don't, who will? When we pray we open the door for God to work in the earth realm. Remember that man still has the lease here. There should be zero stress on us about any of these things. His burden is light. God will show us what He wants us to be involved in.

We can replace those wasted hours with better television options. I really saw my life change when I started watching the *Joseph Prince* broadcast every day. You can find his current show schedule at www.josephprince.org. I get to soak in God's grace and love every day. Believe me, you need it each and every day. I also highly recommend the show *Gary Keesee Fixing the Money Thing*. You can find Gary Keesee's show schedule at www.faithlifenow.com. He does an amazing job talking about God's Kingdom in all areas of life. Another good option is a program called *It's Supernatural* with Sid Roth. This program lets you see many of the miraculous things that God is doing around the world today. His website is www.sidroth.org. A recent addition to my viewing list is the *Kim Clement* program. I really enjoy watching that one online at www.kimclement.tv. Kim provides unique insight into how God is moving today and what is to come in the future. These programs will drastically change your thinking and help your life head in the right direction. So set your DVR and start taking dominion in your life. Replace your wasted hours of television with something that will actually change your life. I'm proof!

Along with television, think of the magazines you read. Think of seemingly harmless magazines such as sports or fashion magazines. Do you really need to have that much knowledge about the inner workings of your favorite team? What will your intense knowledge of sports do to change your life? Nothing at all. What will knowing what your favorite movie star wore to an award ceremony do to change your life? Nothing at all. Tear down those weeds growing in your life and plant something productive with that time.

I think most people just want a break from the fallen world in which they live. Being immersed in it makes you want some relief. I absolutely get that. Keeping yourself distracted may feel good for a little while, but until you come into the Kingdom that feeling is only temporary. You must make the changes that free you from that world's system in order to truly enjoy life.

> You must make the changes that free you from the world's system in order to truly enjoy life.

I suggest replacing those magazines with some great books. A good place to start is with a book called *The Kingdom of God in You* by Bill Winston. He also has another great book called *The Law of Confession* that talks about the power of our words. Other favorites are Joseph Prince's two books *Destined to Reign* and *Unmerited Favor*. John Sheasby's book *The Birthright*, which I mentioned earlier, is also wonderful. If you want to read a book about God's Kingdom as it relates to your finances, read Gary Keesee's *Fixing the Money Thing*. I also really like Brenda Kunneman's book *The Supernatural You* and Harold Hill's *How to Live Like a King's Kid*. So pick up some great books and start taking dominion in your mind!

You also can use the time in your car to listen to teaching on CD or on your iPod. Constantly refreshing your mind with God's Word and with Jesus-centered teaching puts you in a great position to take dominion in your life each day. Talk radio and pop music won't change your life. Transform those wasted hours and help your day to function at a higher level. You can find many great teachings for free on iTunes. Just search for your favorite pastor or teacher and download the free podcasts and try them out. I download John Sheasby's podcast each month. These ministries also have many great CD series available.

Don't forget to work in some quiet time during your day. Shut off the CDs and the TV and put down the book. Just rest and relax and be with your heavenly Daddy. Let Him speak to you. You've asked Him for answers, but often you and I don't settle down enough to hear the answers when they come. That's why many answers come in the night or during other restful times. Also keep in mind that the answers and ideas that come to you may sound really strange. Look into them before you dismiss them. Write them down. If the answer were straightforward you probably would have already done it. God's answers and ideas are literally out of this world.

Guard Your Time

As you can probably already see, an extremely important area to take dominion in is your time. From the President of the United

States to a newborn baby, we each have twenty-four hours a day to operate with. How will you spend those hours? That time is extremely valuable. You are either growing as a person or moving backwards. Thankfully, as a son or daughter of God each of those hours is blessed and you have the favor of God in them.

Consider ways to leverage the limited hours you have. How can you use systems or hire people to make better use of your time? Is it worth your time to mow your lawn and clean your house? Do the analysis. Once you start living at a higher level you will need to see if those hours can be used more productively somewhere else. You get the added benefit of blessing someone else with a job in the process.

As you get older you will value time more because you know there is less and less of it. Time may seem to be going by more quickly, but really it's just that you are more aware of the value of each of those seconds as they tick off the clock. Enjoy the time you have and do something significant with it!

One of the best ways to spend your time is in relationship with those you love. This includes your heavenly Dad. Spend time talking to Him. Attend a church that shows you God's love and reveals Jesus each and every week. There are more and more of them sprouting up each day. This is an exciting time. I have seen things change so much in a very short amount of time.

Also, take time for your spouse and children. Just taking the time to be with them is all they need. You don't always have to be doing something together. Just enjoy each other's company. Build each other up. Bless them with your words all the time. Speak blessings over them. A family that is built upon Christ is on an unshakeable foundation. It's the best place to be as we see the world being shaken.

Also, take the time to take care of the home and the other property you have. If you haven't taken dominion over your home, it will be hard to pay it off. If you don't take care of it, you won't see the value in paying it off early. Have the nicest yard in your neighborhood. Have the cleanest car in the neighborhood. Don't make it an obsession—make it a result of who you are. You are a child of the King. Your life should reflect excellence in all areas.

Taking Dominion in Your Life

As you start taking dominion in each area of your life you will see your life start to change. Years of ignoring things or letting things pile up takes some time to correct. Relax and rest. Give yourself a break and don't stress about it. You only have one choice: move forward or stay where you are. Just take a step and move forward.

CHAPTER 11

Walking Out Success

So now you have your vision and your plan. You have prepared and you are taking dominion. Now it is time to walk out success. You do so through the day-to-day activities and steps that you take on your journey to reach your vision. God says He will bless the work of your hands. If you don't put your hands to anything He won't have anything to bless. When you put your hands to your vision, He will bless it.

I like to think of it as being content with where you are, but always moving forward. If you always focus on tomorrow you will never enjoy today. Today is all there is. I lived that way for years and years, even though my wife tried to wake me up. I always dreamed of the mythical tomorrow where everything was great and life was wonderful. I never realized that if I always lived in tomorrow, then I never actually enjoy today. Thankfully, I finally took her advice and began to maximize each day while enjoying it at the same time. While doing our best each day, with our vision in hand, we walked out success each and every day in the direction of that vision. We weren't striving but resting and moving forward. Today we enjoy the benefits of that diligence and look forward to our next vision.

I also like to call this "one-step success". Your success is wrapped up in the next single step you take. Everything else is attempting to distract you from that next step. That step is either taking you closer to God and your vision or further away from God and your vision. You never actually stand still. You are either advancing or retreating. I found that as you rest in the finished work of Jesus you advance. When you try to push forward in your own power you retreat.

I'm not a big fan of multitasking either. I think you dilute your focus and your power regarding the issue at hand. It might just be a guy thing because my wife is much better at doing several things at once. I try to give a hundred percent to the item right in front of me. I resolve it and move on. So don't have a bunch of outstanding issues sitting in the back of your mind. Jesus always had time for those who came to Him. He was always at rest. People had His complete attention.

You have probably also heard that you should take on your hardest or biggest challenge first. That may be good advice too. It might end up being easier than you think and give you momentum for the next task. Once that giant falls the smaller ones look much easier. You are a champion created to conquer things that aren't right in your life. You and God together are an unstoppable team—the size of the problem is insignificant compared to the size of our God.

Be Led

The easiest way to take your next step is to be directed by the Holy Spirit. The best way to know which step to take is whether you feel peace or don't feel peace about the direction you are moving. If you have peace, you know it is the right direction. If not, it is the wrong direction. I describe the wrong direction as a feeling of sandpaper. When I start to move in the wrong direction it just scrapes my spirit. If it is the right direction, I have peace, even if in the natural that move would seem unwise. Big steps in the right direction often seem scary. That doesn't mean it is the wrong direction. It likely means it is the right direction. If it feels uncomfortable, but you still have peace, it is probably the way to go.

So take a few steps and start moving. Allow the peace of God to direct you along the path. Don't worry so much about the final destination; just focus on the next step you are taking. Relax and rest knowing that God has you in His hands. He'll let you learn along the way, but He will not let you fall.

> Take a few steps and start moving.

There is a big difference between striving under your own power and being led. It takes some practice, but you will learn to know the difference. Stress is a key indicator. If you are stressed and exhausted by the direction you are moving, then it is likely you are striving in your own power. If you are uncomfortable but at peace, you are likely moving in the right direction. (Any of us who are taking territory and expanding our dominion will feel the same way.) You will also receive refreshing along the correct path—something you won't receive on the wrong path.

Stay Open

When you live in God's Kingdom your answer can come in many forms. You might receive a miracle on the spot. You might receive a miracle over a period of time. The answer might pop into your head or it may slowly develop as you move toward your destiny. Don't try to limit God by expecting your answer to show up in only one way.

Many times God will provide your answer through people. Listen to their words. See if the Holy Spirit gives weight to what they are saying. Does what they are saying match up to what you believe God is saying to you? Is He confirming it through another believer?

Change is hard, but it is always necessary to get where you want to be. I like being comfortable—we all do—but that's not an option for growth. I consider myself a rather private person. I typically don't like sharing the details of my life. I realize, though, that I need to put myself out there to grow. It's not always comfortable and it's not always fun, but I am always glad I did it. So while I enjoy writing, sharing this book with others is a stretch for me. It's not comfortable, but it is necessary for me to grow. The same is true for you. Stepping into a state of being uncomfortable is where you will grow.

I mentioned this before, but having a vision and a plan allows you to know what direction you should be heading. If you find yourself stuck, looking for your next step and asking what to do next, come back to your vision. Step back into your state of rest and ask yourself, "What is my priority?" Doing so will take the pressure off in the situation.

There are also situations where you might be stuck for a reason. It may not be the right season to take the step you are about to take. I receive a number of different scriptural e-mail messages in my inbox each day. Sometimes I will go to open one and just don't feel like doing it. It doesn't feel right. My mind is saying I need to read it, but my spirit is saying no. So I don't read it. Days later something will happen in my life and I will be prompted to check the e-mail I didn't read. It will be exactly what I needed to hear at that moment.

Find Support

Try to have people in your life who will encourage you. Your loving heavenly Father and Jesus your Savior should be the foundation of your support. Jesus said the Holy Spirit is our Comforter. We need Him in our daily walk. Your spouse should be the first person you turn to. He or she is your other half. Your spouse is the part of you that forms a complete and wonderful human life together. I couldn't walk any of this out without my wife. She is always encouraging and willing to take the next step in our lives, even when I am hesitant. Parents and friends are a good source too. Mine have been a great support in my life.

I also have mentors who helped direct me on the path. Watching *Joseph Prince* daily and soaking in the encouragement I receive has been extraordinary. The things I have learned and the change in me is amazing. Not only is it like being showered with grace every day, but Pastor Prince does an amazing job of teaching the Bible and revealing Jesus throughout the Old Testament. Gary Keesee is another mentor of mine. Without his teaching and that of his wife Drenda, I doubt we would be debt-free right now. As you can see, some of the best mentors aren't necessarily people you actually interact with or know personally. It's great if you can have some like that also. The best thing is that these virtual mentors are available to you in the comfort of your own home, on your television or on your iPod.

Obstacles in Your Way

An area I had trouble with in the past was excellence versus perfection. My goal before learning about the Kingdom of God was perfection in my daily walk. I was walking the path of self-effort. This greatly impacted my activities. While God is perfect, it is a futile effort on our part to make perfection our goal. Christ is our perfection and we have Him, but I tried to be perfect in my daily life. This came through in my behavior and actions. It is a part of self-righteousness. Thankfully, I have been able to let that go. My goal now is excellence. I don't sweat the details, I rest in Him and I try to perform everything with excellence. If I strove for perfection with this book, it would never be completed.

What is in front of you at this moment? What are you facing? There will be obstacles in your path. There will be mountains in front of you. The Israelites had giants to face and so will you. When you start taking territory, you will encounter resistance. As you start moving toward your vision, you will face opposition. There will be voices that say it's not worth the price. You might also find that it looks much more challenging than you thought

Overflowing Success

it would. This is completely normal and to be expected. In a way, you can get excited when you see opposition pop-up. It means you are heading the right way. Likely nobody will try to stop you if you are sitting still or moving in a direction that won't have an impact. Just know that opposition is coming and know that God will show you the way.

A common enemy we all meet is fear. Fear and worry pave the road to a defeated life. Many in the world and sadly many believers spend much of their time in fear. Fear is the opposite of faith. Fear freezes us in our tracks. Fear is designed to keep us from moving forward and taking territory. It is the basis for all of the obstacles we see and most of it is based in condemnation. It tries to make us feel unworthy to take territory or succeed. We know that there is no condemnation to those who are in Christ Jesus. Hopefully you have received that in your spirit. Your value and position in the Kingdom is unshakeable. So better than fearing less is being entirely fear-free in Christ!

> Your value and position in the Kingdom is unshakeable.

As we were paying off our mortgage, we decided that I should get braces on my teeth. I was in my late thirties but had always wanted straight teeth. One of the things that held me back was that I was told I would need to have my jaw broken and reset. Needless to say I didn't like the idea of breaking my jaw. We prayed about it and found another option: a new surgery where a surgeon tricks the jaw into thinking it is broken. As it heals itself, the teeth move more quickly and things can be put into proper alignment. It was an answer to prayer. My jaw would not have to be broken and I would get the straight teeth I was searching for. The teeth straightening would also be completed in record time. I felt like the Holy Spirit was saying this was the right direction.

As the surgery got closer I was overcome with fear. I would have panic attacks in the middle of the night. Thoughts of "why are you doing this?" would enter my mind. I couldn't sleep during many of the nights leading up to the surgery. This is crazy,

I thought. I have gotten by with my teeth for years, why do this now? Why am I volunteering to do this to my body?

God doesn't want us to just get by, but my attitude was one of "I'm just going to do it scared. I'll keep my head down, push through and it will be worth it when it is over." Anytime we do something new or push into new territory it is scary, but it is necessary for growth. Most of the time your fear is never realized. Just remember Who is with you. He has promised to never leave you or forsake you.

What I discovered is that God's best for us is not being afraid and pushing through. Pushing through in fear is better than standing still in fear, but God wants more for us. Jesus is our example. We have been redeemed through Christ and are now sons. Sons of the King do not need to merely survive or get through a situation. Sadly, I feel this is the way many look at life. They are surviving the pain and will get to heaven some day. Although it might sound spiritual, this is actually a focus on a fear of death. Death has been destroyed. We can rest. Survival until death is no way to live. We are alive in Christ right now. We are able to live the abundant life both now and for eternity. As I said, God's will according to the Lord's prayer is that His will be done on earth as it is in heaven. So today, right now, in your situation, He wants heaven to be released. In heaven there is no pain. In heaven there is no fear or worry. That is how He wants it to be in your life right now. So rest in His perfect love for you and it will cast out all of the fear in your life. When you know how much He loves you, what can scare you?

CHAPTER 12

Bring on the Giants

I mentioned earlier – how I read a lot of books about worldly success when I was trying to succeed the world's way. One of the books that I read was *Awaken the Giant Within* by Tony Robbins. It is considered to be a classic motivational book concerning success and changing your mindset. I definitely like the book and it was one that I decided to keep when I was giving many of those books away. There are many powerful ideas in that book. He dedicates an entire chapter to talking about the importance of your belief system. Another one of my favorite motivational authors, Jim Rohn, refers to your belief system as your philosophy. I completely agree with the importance of your belief system. I think most people, though, have a belief system solely based on themselves and their effort. That's doomed to failure. I also think many people base their belief system on religion. They believe, like I once did, that success would come because they are a good person. They are hoping that because of their performance God will show up in their situation.

I believe that *Overflowing Success* reveals the ultimate belief system and philosophy for life. It is a belief system based on everything already being provided through Christ—a system based on resting in that finished work. God's Kingdom really is the source of all your success and the only true power that releases real success in your life.

Let's stick with the idea of giants for this final chapter. In the Bible we see that giants are the bad guys; they are things that stand in the way of your destiny. So I definitely didn't want to awaken a giant within me or to become a giant at all. Giants can be those things that look like success under the "earth curse" system. It's all about self-effort. Many have done all they can to become giants themselves. By this I mean they are trying to succeed the world's way. They are trying to make themselves bigger and stronger than the competition. They are sacrificing everything to gain what they think will make them happy, only to be disappointed when they get there.

The real giants in your life can be anything negative. Giants are the problems in your life. They are the barriers to your success. They can be disease, being overweight, a lost job, a broken relationship, financial problems; they are just about anything that keeps you from enjoying God's best in your life right now. Obviously these problems seem daunting if you choose to focus on them. A giant looks bigger the more you look at him.

My suggestion is that instead of awakening the giant within, awaken the giant defeating champion within. God's Kingdom is in you right now. God has created you to defeat every giant you come into contact with. You have that power available. He has made you more than a conqueror. He has created you to be a champion. He has also promised to never leave you, so He is with you in every conflict.

David's Example

David in the Bible is the most obvious example of someone who awoke the giant defeating champion within. It was easy to see his giant. The giant was standing right in front of him and the children of Israel and taunting them each and every day. David didn't have to wonder what his giant was. I'm sure that some of you have experienced taunting by a giant!

Bring on the Giants

The children of Israel sat back waiting for a miracle. They knew their God had provided for them in the past. When they didn't see that miracle show up, they tried to figure out a solution in the natural world, just like many do today. Obviously they didn't have anyone on their side who matched up with that giant pound for pound. Success didn't seem to be an option at all. They took their eyes off their God and put them on their problem.

David had a different mindset than the rest of the children of Israel, though. So David became their solution. He knew that they had a covenant and that God was with them. He didn't see the giant as much of a problem at all. He saw him as an opportunity—an opportunity to leave the shepherd world and to move into the royal world he already knew he was destined to be a part of. He saw an opportunity to see his nation succeed. Goliath was an opportunity to show the world the God of Israel.

You need to have a David kind of mindset—a giant defeating champion mindset. David knew who he was and who his God was. He had relationship with Him—the kind of relationship that let David know that he wasn't alone in this battle. It was the kind of relationship that caused him to run toward the battle instead of standing on the sidelines. He already knew he had the victory before he got into the battle. He knew it would work; he had seen it work before. God was with him when he defeated the bear and the lion previously. The result would be no different this time.

This is the same mindset that Joshua and Caleb had when they spied out the land. They saw the giants as being easy to deal with since they had God with them. The other spies left God out of the equation and looked only at the size of the giants. Many are doing the same thing with their giants today. Joshua and Caleb looked at the size of their God instead, just as we need to.

Cultivating a David Mindset

So how do you cultivate a David kind of mindset? Step number one is to believe that God is and that He is a rewarder of those who seek Him. By reading this book and using the other tools I mention, you are heading down the correct path. You reach that place of belief by doing the things we have already covered. You change your heart and guard your heart. You change the words that you speak over your life. You change the things that you watch and listen to.

Start sowing God's Word into your heart. His words change your thinking and change your belief about what is truly possible in your life. I like to search on www.BibleGateway.com for key words that I want to meditate on, such as success, prosperity, blessing and favor in the Bible. I then copy and paste the scriptures that I find onto a sheet so I can use them to meditate on. I cannot emphasize enough the need to speak God's Word aloud. This is true meditation. I mutter those scriptures and draw out their spiritual nutrients throughout the day. Proverbs would be another great set of scriptures to speak aloud throughout the day. There are many testimonials and even books written about the success people have received by meditating on Proverbs.

The great news for us is that we have an even better covenant than David had. If David had success with giants, then we should have even greater success with them. But to do that you must believe that you are a son or daughter of our heavenly Father. You must believe that you are a member of the royal family. You must believe that you can reign in life. Meditate on how loved you are by God. Start thinking throughout the day how precious you are to Him and the price that was paid to free you from darkness. Soak in His love for you. This can take minutes or months. Write down those scriptures that remind you of this truth and read them aloud each day. Speaking God's Word over yourself is definitely a key to overflowing success.

You must also believe that you are an entirely new creation—a creation free of the "earth curse," a unique creation of our loving Father. Your success is based on your Daddy and your heavenly family. It isn't based on you anymore. You are an ambassador for your Dad's Kingdom here on the earth. As a child of the King your life represents success. Now you need to look at everything in life through this new point of view. Nothing is impossible to the son or daughter of the King.

Bring on the Giants

As a child of the King your life represents success.

Before success comes and can overflow, you need to believe. You need to believe what God says about you and that you are established. Believe that you are established in His grace, established in His love, established in your position in the family. You need to be comfortable with your solid position in Christ. If you aren't, then the success won't come. You won't feel worthy and you won't pull heaven into this world.

Be sure not to use your emotions as an indicator in your life. Your emotions can lead you astray. Regardless of how you feel, it does not change what Christ has done for you. Regardless of how large that giant looks, he is already defeated. Whether or not you feel successful at this moment means nothing. When you know who you are and whose you are, you know that nothing is impossible. You have a new belief system. It's not one based on emotions, but one based on love—His love for you.

The thing we must realize is that David's success wasn't just for David. His success overflowed into the entire nation. Everyone benefited from David's faith. Everyone benefited from David stepping onto that battlefield. His victory benefited generations. Your victory will benefit others too. It will benefit your family, your church, your community and your world. You're not defeating the giant for your sake only.

People are extremely interested in your victory. They are really interested in your success. They are also interested in your fruit. It draws them in for a closer look. They want to taste the fruit of God in your life. When they do, they will see that it is good. They will want that fruit in their life. When your success overflows you start sowing good things in the lives of others. You pass along books that speak to you. You pass along CDs of teachings that you think will help others.

As you probably know by now, these giants won't be too hard to find. They always show up when you are moving toward your destiny, but they can even show up when you are minding your own business and hiding from your destiny. So living below your potential doesn't keep a giant from showing up.

I break down these giants into two categories. I call one a pop-up giant and the other a squatter giant. A pop-up giant comes at you from out of the blue. It reveals itself as you are moving through life. A squatter giant is residing in the area of your promised land. He is a squatter in an area God has given to you for your destiny.

Dealing with a Pop-Up Giant

Many times what you need is a quick solution to an immediate situation. You are moving through life and a giant pops up. Instead of using a sword or javelin, he throws a wrench into your day. It could be a broken down car, a lost item, a storm heading toward you or the need for a close parking spot. These are situations that require a solution right now. They need success this very moment.

In these situations you are already resting in who you are. You don't get upset. The giant doesn't cause panic. You come at these problems from a relaxed position, resting in Christ. With that as your starting point, you fully expect heaven to show up in that situation. You fully expect a miracle to occur at that very moment.

Your weapon with which to fight this giant is what you believe in your heart and what you speak with your mouth. This is the slingshot and the stone that will drop the giant. You are fully persuaded in your victory before you step out in faith. This happens by what we have learned throughout this book.

If it is something like a lost item, simply speak out loud something like this: "Thank You, Dad, that we find our lost item in the next half hour." Then remain relaxed and rest. Don't search on your own. Don't do anything in your own strength. You have taken it out of your hands. You have placed it in His hands. Your situation is now under His Kingdom and dominion. You are depending on Him for your answer and waiting for that answer to come. The answer could come in any form. It could be a picture in your mind. It could be a leading to head a certain direction. It could be a strange thought. It could be an old friend calling you out of the blue.

Bring on the Giants

For me, many times, it seems like my thought, but it has a slightly different feel to it. It's hard to describe. It has a different texture to it. It stands out. Sometimes it appears as a picture in my mind, but different than just imagining something. It will probably seem different to each of you, but you will start to sense it more easily over time. Assume that the thoughts that come are from God and that your answer is contained in them.

For something like a strong storm coming your way, say out loud something like this: "This storm shall not come near my home, in Jesus' name. Storm, you have no right to come near my home. My home and family will not be harmed; we are covered in the blood of Jesus." As before, you remain at rest. You're not stopping the storm; you've spoken to the storm based on your position in Him and the right He gave you to use His name. You just go about your business. You are focused on Him and His love for you, not on the storm. The storm is insignificant in relation to Him.

I've heard people who are successful in praying for the sick say that they may have prayed for hundreds of people before people began to be healed. Now many or most are healed when they pray. In the same way you need to put yourself out there to be successful. You have to step out in faith. You have to be willing to look foolish. You have to be willing to step on the battlefield, against a giant, in front of two armies, with no armor on and a slingshot in your hand. I've prayed and spoken things many times in front of people that I know sound crazy to them. I've received my share of strange looks, especially from other believers.

I know that speaking to a storm seems foolish to your natural mind. However, it's not your mind that's stopping the storm. It's not you who's doing anything at all. The pressure is one hundred percent off you to succeed in this situation. You are just speaking from your authority in Him. He is doing it. Your part is to believe Him. It's Kingdom business. It's royal family business. That storm or whatever giant you are facing is part of the earth curse system and is dark and destructive. Anything dark has zero authority or ability to affect your life unless you choose to allow it.

Too many times we think we are just in a completely random state of existence. We just deal with things as they bump into us each day. That's not truly living! We must wake up the giant defeating champion within us. We must realize that God's Kingdom is already in us. We must wake up from our slumber and realize that as a new creation these things have no say in our life.

Dealing with a Squatter Giant

Some other giants in your life will require a process in order to defeat them. Those squatters in your promised land will require you to make some changes in your life and will take some time to defeat. Thankfully time can be compressed and our success can come more quickly through God's Kingdom. And, as we know, change isn't always fun. However, just as with the pop-up giants, when defeating squatter giants we must start from a position of knowing who we are and of believing that God's Kingdom is backing us up. Jesus gave us that authority. His Kingdom is in us and we are resting in Him and what He has done for us.

These longer-term situations could be things such as weight loss, meeting your future spouse, finding a new job, starting a successful business, having a baby, etc. This is not to say that an instant miracle can't happen to bring these things into your life. That's completely possible and should be your expected starting point. However, these are the areas in your life that the Kingdom of God isn't dominating currently. These giants are squatting on the areas where you need heaven on earth—where you need heaven to show up in a specific situation.

We reach success in these areas by doing the things we have already covered for the pop-up giants: knowing who we are and whose we are. With that as our base we come up with our vision and our plan. Then we move toward that vision being led by the Holy Spirit and taking territory and dominion day by day.

The vision you receive comes from the Kingdom of God within you. Your heart knows what God has placed in it for your future. It's okay to receive some input from your senses, but make sure you check what you receive against your heart. Even those people of the world know it is best to go with your "gut" over your head.

Bring on the Giants

All of us have been made in God's image, so we all still have that ability.

Your answer is going to sound strange. Go after a giant with a slingshot? That doesn't sound right. Invest in a credit card company during the banking crisis? Are you sure about this, God? Success comes when you stop looking for the logical solution and look for the heavenly solution. That solution will sound strange to you. You must have faith enough to receive it and to act on it.

> Success comes when you stop looking for the logical solution and look for the heavenly solution.

The giant's defeat will also require boldness. People of the world know that if they want to see success they have to take it for themselves. They know they have to be bold and conquer something to win. We too need to be bold—not bold based on ourselves, but bold based on the Kingdom backing us up. We are to be bold based on our Father's love for us; bold based on Jesus' sacrifice that restored us; bold based on direction from the Holy Spirit. Worldly success comes to many who are bold. Overflowing success, though, only comes to those who are bold in Him.

Defeating a squatter giant also requires patience. When I first stepped out and started writing this book I took a week off and started writing. I had the bulk of the book completed in that week. That was a year and a half ago. I thought I was ready to have the book in your hands. I started moving forward and trying to get it published and into the marketplace. Everything I tried fell short. I felt like I was hitting a brick wall. I kept running into dead ends. In the meantime I kept making changes and updating the book. What seemed complete to me at that point seems very incomplete looking back on it.

I had asked God for direction for the book from the time I started writing. By "direction" I meant getting the book completed and in the marketplace. Not much was coming to me in that area. Then one day I was in the shower and asked God again to give me direction on what to do next with the book. That same day I received an online request to reconnect with someone I went to college with. I was excited to find out that she did book publishing for exactly this kind of book.

I realize now that that first week wasn't the season for this book yet. I wasn't ready and this book wasn't ready. I had to be patient and enjoy the rest of my life while moving my vision for the book forward to its completion. The same can be said for you. Many times when we step out we are expecting something to arrive that very moment. Have patience. The end result will be much better.

Conclusion

When we first became new parents we would routinely ask other parents questions about babies. We would ask different people how they would handle different situations. Most of the time we would receive very different answers. As we discovered, each baby is unique and each phase for each baby is unique. I'm going to say something similar to you as we end this book. Each of you is unique and each season of your life is unique. Your overflowing success is going to be unique to you and to the season you are in.

The one thing that will be consistent in all of your success is rest. Resting in Jesus' finished work on the cross. Resting in God's grace. This is the only way to experience overflowing success in your life. This is the only way to step into your destiny. Until you enter that land of rest everything you do will be in vain. Rest and be free of self-effort and self-righteousness. Rest and be free of fear, worry and stress.

I have really enjoyed taking this journey with you. This book contains many of the success concepts that have worked in my life and that I know will work in yours. We've reached the point where it's time for you to invest what you have learned. Think of this as harvesting your success. What do I mean? In the earth you sow seed and the seed starts growing and receives water. The sun shines on it and eventually that seed grows into a plant. That plant contains more seed that can be used to grow an entire field.

That original seed in fact contained within it enough future seed and crops to cover the entire planet. An amazing result from just one small seed!

Sow Seed, Harvest Success

Your part in overflowing success is to sow seed in your life and to harvest the success that grows from it. You are doing that already with the concepts we have covered. Sure, you might have to knock down some weeds (or giants) now and then, but nearly all the work falls on God. He created the seed and He created you. God created the vast crop within that seed and He created the vast potential within you. He provides the soil, the sun and the rain. He provides the seasons. He provided everything that you have to work with and create with. He provided your skills and your talents. Your job is to recognize that if you don't invest what He has provided, you don't receive a harvest. So sow your seed and keep your vision for the harvest. Relax in God's finished work and be ready to harvest in the right season.

As I've said, your harvest of success is dependent on the things we have covered already. What do you have dominion over? What is your vision? Let's take an example. Does your current job (where you have dominion) have the capability to get you to where you want to be (your vision)? God might have to move you to a new position or a new company or prompt you to start your own business to reach your vision (your harvest). The change that takes place to get you where you need to be can be unsettling. That's okay. It will be worth it.

I am sure it's no coincidence that man was placed in a garden at the very beginning. That garden was a finished work of God. Man just needed to rest and enjoy that finished work. We are also in a finished work—a superior finished work. It is the finished work of Christ on the cross. We too are to rest and enjoy that finished work.

You are sowing seeds in your life all the time. Sadly, most of the world is sowing seeds of doubt, depression, anger and selfishness in their life. They sow seeds with their words and their expectations. They also sow them by what they watch and what they listen to.

Conclusion

They water those seeds nonstop and then are surprised when they find those negative things growing in their life. They don't have to look too far for that harvest. It shows up right under their nose.

Sowing negative seeds can also be seen in self-effort. They are a result of self-righteousness, the working of the flesh. The opposite of this is bearing fruit. Bearing fruit is producing good results in your life. Bearing fruit is real success. This is not a result of works but of rest. A tree doesn't have to do anything but be itself to bear fruit. It's not a struggle and it's not hard work. When you are relaxed and being your true self you are producing fruit and you are producing overflowing success.

As I have said, the main thing you sow in your heart to achieve overflowing success is the Word of God. You sow seed that allows you to really know God, that lets you know that He isn't a hard taskmaster, and that tells you He is your loving Father. That allows you to receive the relationship He wants to have with you. So you sow seed in your heart through the things you read and the things you listen to. You are also sowing seed with your words, your thoughts and your expectations.

The purpose of this entire book is to get you to the point where you have sown so much in your heart that success is what naturally flows out of you. You must have your faith at a point where nothing seems impossible to you. You don't want to start building your faith when a giant pops up. You don't want to start building your faith when a problem arises. You want to have it built up well before anything comes along. So the time to build it up is right now. Start this moment and consistently add to it. When the time comes, it will be natural to succeed. Success takes over your thinking. Your spirit is running the show again. You check your heart, you know what you believe and you act on that belief.

You want to have your faith built up well before anything comes along.

There are even times when you might need to sow a specific financial seed that you harvest in the future. You can sow your finances into a ministry in God's Kingdom and then later receive the harvest that you need. You might also sow your time into a ministry where you see results. In this case, look for ministries that are affecting people's lives and achieving success in the area you need success in. If you need weight loss you might sow into a ministry where there are numerous testimonies of weight loss. Ask the Holy Spirit where to sow and what to sow.

After you sow, be on the lookout for your harvest—not from outside but from the Kingdom of God within you. As I have said many times, what you need likely won't show up on your doorstep. God will give you glimpses of your harvest. He will show you which step to take next along the path to success. Be looking with your eyes but mainly with your heart. God will give you ideas, concepts, direction, favor, blessing and divine appointments on the way to your success. Your job is to be ready and to receive them when they appear. So simply walk in the direction that God gives you.

Take Action

By now I know that you can see the amazing possibilities for your life. Your amazing harvest is waiting for you. You are on your way to a completely transformed life—a life of health, happiness, peace, joy, loving relationships and solid finances. I hope you see that absolutely everything is possible in Christ.

Do you have your vision and your plan written down? Remember, the check isn't coming in the mail. Your success requires action. Whether it is financial freedom, better relationships or a new career, it is available in God's Kingdom. Whatever it is, it will likely be more simple to achieve than you think. The steps to overflowing success can be pretty basic. That doesn't mean it will always be easy, though. Change never is.

When you reach your first vision, move on to another. That vision doesn't have to be the end of your journey. There is always that next frontier. What you have learned from seeing overflowing success in action you can apply in every area of life.

Conclusion

Even if you spend all of your time, money and energy becoming the most successful person you can in your own strength, there is a whole other side to you that is being neglected. It is the spiritual side. I don't mean just going to church or reading your Bible. I mean a real spiritual life that begins to overshadow the reality of this world. I mean a personal relationship with our Savior Jesus Christ in which every day you talk and laugh and enjoy each other. I mean a personal relationship with our loving heavenly Daddy—a relationship based on His perfect love for us and His wanting the absolute best for us now and throughout eternity. I mean an amazing daily interaction with the Holy Spirit, receiving the direction you need and miraculous support in your daily life.

You will discover that there is a price for everything in life. There is a price you have to pay to change and grow. There is also a price to pay for staying where you are. It is the price of knowing you wasted many years sitting in fear and never taking action. I hope you know that the only price worth paying is the price of success. It is the price you must pay to grow and change. God is all about success. His Kingdom is all about success and He wants His children to succeed. Our lives should reflect His glory. He will help you!

God is all about success.

You will lose something in this process. You will lose your old self when you enter the Kingdom of God. The weights of this world that are keeping you down will have to go. The attitudes that have kept you in bondage will have to go. In fact, you won't look much like you did before you entered His Kingdom. You will be a completely new you—a new creation. You will be a happier, shinier, more successful and bolder version of you.

The only time you will have the faith to grow and change is when you know who you are and whose you are. This allows you to rest and receive success in your life. This allows you to receive success that is truly supernatural. This allows you to bear abundant fruit in your life. This allows success to overflow in your life.

Overflowing Success

With your life set on the unshakeable foundation of Christ you will stand while others shake. While others fear, you will rest in the arms of your loving Father. You will flourish while others run for cover. The problems of this world become opportunities for you as a son or daughter of the King.

Always remember that everyone has the right to this relationship with God. The Bible says God is no respecter of persons. This means what He has done for us, He will do for everyone, and even greater things. I hear and see amazing things happening in people's lives all the time.

Jesus paid the price for everyone to enter this Kingdom. You don't need to clean people up or change their behavior. Just tell them the good news and share what God has done in your life. Show them your fruit. Show them your success. Your friends are looking for reality. They aren't interested in going through the motions of religion. They are looking for the answers you are discovering. People need to see the success of God in your life!

Take the time to learn all you can about God's Kingdom. It truly is priceless. I have only dipped my toe into these waters. I wish I had done it sooner, but I know there is nothing to gain by looking backward. The past doesn't exist anymore. I can only focus on the present, just like you. I want to keep growing and learning; I want to keep gaining a deeper relationship with God and helping others to do the same. When you have amazing things happen to you in your life, share them. Tell as many people as you can what God has done for you in your life!

As I mentioned, this relationship with God not only corrects your financial situation and your relationships, but it also makes everything in your life come together. You become unstuck! You start to see how life should be lived. God's Kingdom produces life. It brings life to absolutely every situation.

You will notice something when you read the Bible. You will also notice it when you hear someone's amazing testimony. The thing you will notice is that overflowing success is a combination of God and us. We all know God can do all things. But we tend to forget that His Word says that we can do all things. Listen to that again. We can do all things through Christ. That means we

Conclusion

are involved. It is His power that causes miracles. It is His power that transforms lives. But His power flows through people into the earth realm. We tend to forget that all of the amazing stories in the Bible involve people—people believing God; people who stepped out of the boat; people who placed their hands on someone to heal that person. All of the amazing stories going on in the world today also involve people.

Not everyone believed God enough to enter the promised land. Not everyone believed God enough to take out Goliath. They all had the opportunity. They looked at the opportunity and said that they couldn't do it. They didn't awaken the giant defeating champion within. They looked at the situation instead of at their God. The odds probably won't appear to be in your favor either. That's okay. Someone has to believe God enough to take that step. That's where you come in.

Overflowing success is allowing yourself to be God's access point to bless others. You are blessed to be a blessing. Open yourself up to Him and say yes. Say that you will allow yourself to be a conduit. You will be God's access point to bring heaven into the earth realm. God is your senior partner in your destiny. That destiny is transforming your life and the lives of others. God loves people! He loves us so much He already gave us the answer to everything. You have already found that answer. His name is Jesus.

About the Author

Todd R. Weaver lives in Columbus, Ohio with his amazing wife and son. He first experienced God's Kingdom when he was healed of juvenile arthritis as a young boy. Todd received a bachelor's degree from The University of Findlay with a dual major in marketing and business administration. His first piece of writing was nationally published during college. He has spent his career in business to business sales. Todd also enjoys being an entrepreneur. Most of all Todd has a passion for constantly improving life!

www.overflowingsuccess.com

www.toddrweaver.com

Made in the USA
San Bernardino, CA
04 September 2014